Eugène de Mazenod

A Saint for Today

Eugène de Mazenod
A Saint for Today

ALEX R. HEY

Leonine Publishers
Phoenix, Arizona

Copyright © 2017 Alex R. Hey

All rights reserved. No part of this book may be reproduced or transmitted in any form or by any means, electronic or mechanical, including photocopying, recording, or by any information storage or retrieval system now existing or to be invented, without written permission from the respective copyright holder(s), except for the inclusion of brief quotations in a review.

Published by

Leonine Publishers LLC
Phoenix, Arizona, USA

ISBN-13: 978-1-942190-38-7
Library of Congress Control Number: 2017957891

Printed in the United States of America
10 9 8 7 6 5 4 3 2 1

Visit us online at www.leoninepublishers.com
For more information: info@leoninepublishers.com

Table of Contents

Introduction. 1
I. Background 5
II. Into Exile. 15
III. Early Exile 19
IV. Don Bartolo Zinelli 25
V. A Broken Family 35
VI. Separation From Don Bartolo 43
VII. The Cannizzaro Family. 53
VIII. Return to France 61
IX. Spiritual Crisis 67
X. Light Breaks Through 83
XI. Following the Call 89
XII. Purgation 97
XIII. Virtue in the Seminary 109
XIV. Education 119
XV. A Church in Need. 125
XVI. Serving the Most Abandoned. 131
XVII. The Oblates 147
XVIII. Marseilles 157
XIX. Papal Approbation. 163
XX. Abandoned 169
XXI. Bishop of Marseilles. 175
XXII. The Accomplishments of Bishop Eugène
    de Mazenod. 181
XXIII. The Bishop and the Government. 187
XXIV. Gate to the World 191
XXV. Son of Mary 195
XXVI. Death 203
XXVII. Canonization. 205
Epilogue: A Saint for Today 209
Appendix: Prayers. 213
Bibliography. 225

Introduction

My parents divorced when I was three years old. Over the past two decades, I have gotten used to the various inconveniences from having divorced parents, and the divorce is no longer a source of daily anxiety for me. Yet, no matter how much time goes by, the pain never totally goes away. At any moment, a memory could resurface, information previously unknown to me could come to my attention, or someone ignorant of the situation could accidentally say the wrong thing to me. Any one of those scenarios could bring back the pain of my parents' divorce, thrusting me into new turmoil.

In the spring of 2012, I found myself in one of those aforementioned scenarios. The pain could not be ignored, and I went to an adoration chapel, but was unable to pray or to even think. After two hours of just feeling pain, the grace of God broke through, and I was able to leave the chapel and carry on with my life as if nothing had happened.

Even though divorce is quite common, it is easy to feel alone in those moments, and I felt very alone that day in the chapel. I knew I needed an ally, and after leaving the chapel, I conducted a Google search for the patron saint of children of divorced parents. Hours of searching turned up only the patron saint of dysfunctional families whom I ignored because, even though my parents are divorced, my family is not dysfunctional. Yet, after failing to find a patron saint of children of divorced parents, I begrudgingly decided to explore the patron saint of dysfunctional families.

The first thing informational websites usually list under the name and picture of a saint is the day the Church celebrates that particular saint. In the case of Saint Eugène de Mazenod, that day is May 21, my birthday. The first book of Kings tells us that God speaks to us in whispers, but in that moment, God smacked me on the back of the head and shouted, "Are you paying attention?" I could not deny that God wanted me to know Saint Eugène.

Time passed, and I began to grow frustrated that no one knew about this saint with divorced parents. Over the summer, an idea for a book about Saint Eugène and how he dealt with his parents' divorce began to form in my mind. As I began to study his life, I became even more frustrated that the only books about Saint Eugène were out of print and dealt very little with his feelings regarding his parents' divorce, further fueling my desire to write a book about his early life. I soon found out the reason no one had written about his parents was because Eugène wrote little about his parents' divorce.

Yet, as I learned more about Eugène, I began to find similarities between Eugène and myself beyond the divorce of our respective parents. For instance, Eugène struggled with anger, like I do. After reading some of his writings, I often found myself thinking, "I could have written that." When he found himself spending long amounts of time alone with his thoughts, Eugène wrote how "these thoughts go round and round in my head whenever I am alone." I, too, have found being alone with my thoughts a dangerous place to be. He also wrote on more than one occasion of his belief that no one understood him, a feeling I have felt on more than one occasion myself. We even had something so obscure as a dislocated shoulder in common.

These similarities inspired me to dive deeper into his life, and despite not caring about his life after the trauma of his parents' divorce, I found myself learning more and more about

Saint Eugène. He lived an incredible life. At a young age, his family was forced into exile, and while in exile, his parents got divorced. When he returned from exile, his life did not improve the way he thought it would. He overcame the trauma and disappointments of his life to become a priest dedicated to serving the most abandoned in society. Also, Eugène founded the Missionary Oblates of Mary Immaculate and served as bishop of Marseilles, France. His determination and zeal for the salvation of souls inspired me, which increased my frustration that no one knew about him. By the time I was finally able to dedicate myself to telling Saint Eugène's story in early 2015, I had moved on from my original intention of writing about his parents' divorce and decided to tell his whole story because he was not merely a child of divorced parents. Yes, his parents were divorced, but that was not who he was.

Saint Eugène was not defined by his parents' divorce, and in realizing that about him, I realized the same about myself. I am not defined by my parents' divorce or anything bad that has happened to me in my life, nor can the same be said about anyone else. We are not defined by broken families, refugee status, political or religious persecution, abandonment, or any other tragedy. Our identities can only be found in God. This is the sentiment Saint Eugène expressed in his 1813 Ash Wednesday sermon when he told the people of Aix-en-Provence, "You are God's children, the brothers of Jesus Christ, heirs to His eternal kingdom, chosen portion of His inheritance." This was the message I want to spread to others. Amid all of the turmoil facing the world today, the example of Saint Eugène is needed to remind the world of the dignity of every human person.

I

Background

Family

During the late eighteenth century, the French nobility lived lavishly. They felt it was necessary that their lifestyle matched the importance of their class. This was difficult for Charles-Antoine de Mazenod, president at the Court of Accounts, Aids, and Finances of Provence. His salary was insufficient to cover the expenses associated with maintaining the lifestyle expected of him. This created financial restraints that could not be ignored. To remedy this precarious position, thirty-three-year-old Charles-Antoine married eighteen-year-old Marie-Rose Joannis who was not in the nobility, but was from a wealthy bourgeois family. Her dowry would help provide the funds necessary to continue the charade of financial stability in the de Mazenod family, and his social rank would behoove the Joannis family. Charles-Antoine's in-laws would never let him forget that they were the reason he had financial security, and the Joannis family would continue to vex him for the remainder of his life.

Despite the fifteen-year age gap between the spouses and the underlying tension between the de Mazenod and Joannis families, life in Aix was pleasant for Charles-Antoine and Marie-Rose de Mazenod. Their marriage produced three children: Saint Eugène de Mazenod, his older sister Charlotte Élisabeth Eugénie (1779-1784), and his little sister Charlotte Eugénie Antoinette (1785-1867) who was known by the nickname "Ninette." The de Mazenod family lived in a mansion along the Cours Mirabeau, a famous thoroughfare in Aix-en-Provence which was home to many families of the aristocracy. Their life was not perfect, but they were happy and comfortable. The marriage of Charles-Antoine and Marie-Rose would soon be put to the test, however, as Marie-Rose's health began to deteriorate and tensions that had been brewing between the social classes of France for years erupted into revolution, forcing them into exile and poverty.

Anger

Money was not the only reason for Charles-Antoine's distaste for his wife's family. When his son, Eugène, was born on August 1, 1782, the Joannis family had another reason to quarrel with Charles-Antoine. They had conflicting ideas on how the boy ought to be raised. Early in his life, Eugène discovered the phrase "Vuoli!" (I want it). He refused to give up if he did not get what he desired and would resort to using force if necessary. Charles-Antoine was disappointed to see his son exhibiting a character flaw he also possessed and desired to eliminate this behavior early in the child's life before it became a life-long struggle. His father-in-law, Eugène's grandfather, opposed these efforts. Joseph Thomas Joannis liked the idea of his grandson having "a backbone." Sadly, there would be tension over the raising of Saint Eugène de Mazenod for almost all of his formative years which would have a lasting impact on his life.

When young Eugène's temper flared up, the only guaranteed method his family found to calm their young nobleman was to bring him to church. Of this bizarre method of cooling his anger, Eugène wrote:

> God placed in me, I would almost say, a kind of instinct to love Him, my reason was not yet formed when I loved to dwell in His presence, to raise my feeble hands to Him, listen to His word in silence as if I understood it. By nature

lively and irrepressible, it was enough to bring me before the altar to make me gentle and utterly tranquil, so ravished was I by my God's perfections as if by instinct, as I said, for at that age, I did not understand them.

The young nobleman was enamored with the ceremonies he witnessed in church. He sought to imitate them by playing Mass. Eugène would reportedly become displeased if anyone attending one of his make-believe services smiled at the cuteness of his sermons or did not reverently carry out the task he assigned to them. An early biographer related this anecdote about Eugène during the period his family spent living in Venice:

> When he was at home, Eugene could be seen happily dressing himself in an overcoat which looked like a cassock. He would tie up the folds with a belt, place a square biretta on his head and walk up and down in the great hall, known in Venice as *il Portico*, devoutly reciting the office of the Blessed Virgin Mary which he would recite in its entirety every day. Often, he would make his spiritual reading out loud as if he were preaching a sermon. He would do this seated on a large stool which served as his pulpit.

Eugène's early attraction to something he did not understand foreshadows the great love he would one day have for his Creator. However, it was not always feasible for the de Mazenods to bring Eugène to a church to calm him, and Joseph Thomas Joannis' efforts to ensure his grandson had a backbone resulted in Eugène developing a fiery personality that was difficult to tame.

When he was four years old, Eugène attended a theatrical production with his uncles. Because they were in the nobility, they sat in box seats, while the commoners sat below. During the performance, a ruckus broke out below them, disturbing Eugène's enjoyment of the show. Standing on tiptoe to find the source of the commotion, he shouted down to the members of the audience below him, "If I have to come down there!" The sudden outburst from a small child shocked the ringleaders of the disturbance, and they immediately ceased their disruptive behavior.

This struggle with anger plagued Saint Eugène de Mazenod for the entirety of his life. One time while bishop of Marseilles, he was presiding over a solemn liturgy when he noted his vicar general and best friend, Father Henri Tempier, silently praying his breviary. In a hushed tone, Eugène asked him to put his breviary away. A short while later, Tempier still had his breviary, and he was once again quietly told to put it away. When the command was ignored again, Eugène smacked the breviary out of his hands, sending it skittering across the floor, and shouted, "Tempier, what do you take me for, a piece of dog shit?"[1]

A Heart as Big as Saint Paul's, as Big as the World

Despite his well-documented issues with anger, it cannot be said that Eugène de Mazenod had a predominately angry and harsh temperament. On the contrary, he possessed a tremendous amount of compassion. Saint Eugène once declared, "[A]nyone who is suffering, or needs me, can count on my help." Many of his spiritual sons would later report the great compassion and charity he showed to others in the course of his ministry.

The same child who chastised rabble rousers at the theater reported to his spiritual director at Saint Sulpice Seminary that as a child he frequently gave away his breakfast to the poor or brought firewood to people who complained of the cold. On one occasion, young Eugène stopped a boy who was hauling

---

[1] This story was not written down until Alfred Hubenig, O.M.I., included it in his 1995 book *Living in the Spirit's Fire*. Prior to Hubenig's book, it had been passed down as an oral tradition among the Missionary Oblates of Mary Immaculate.

charcoal and traded clothes with him in the street. When he arrived home wearing the charcoal hauler's ragged and grimy clothing, his embarrassed and bewildered mother scolded him, reminding him that he was the son of a president and was expected to maintain a certain standard of appearance. To which the young boy replied, "Very well, I shall be a charcoal-hauler president."

This compassion was the defining characteristic of Saint Eugène de Mazenod. He once remarked, "I live only by the heart." His contemporaries did not point to his anger to describe him. Instead, they noted his abundant compassion. One of his brother bishops described him as having "a heart as big as St. Paul's, as big as the world."

He was keenly aware of his struggles with his temper and apologized immediately upon realizing he had done wrong. "If I let slip some ungracious word, I am as upset as if I had committed a felony…When I had offended someone, even if it was a servant, I never had a moment's peace until I had been able to make reparation for what I had done, with some gifts, or gesture of friendship, or even a hug for the one who had reason to complain about me," he wrote in the self-portrait he composed for the director of his seminary. He knew that he could get carried away by emotion. In the aftermath of one such occasion, he wrote to his father, "God forbid that I should have any intention of causing you pain! When one is passionately in the grip of an idea, one sometimes uses forceful language, words that are not well weighed, well thought out."

One night, the elderly Bishop Eugène de Mazenod sat in his living quarters writing one of his many letters when he heard a knock on his door. "Who is it?" Eugène demanded. When Father Timon-David announced himself, the bishop answered, "Who told you I was here? Can a bishop not get a moment's peace for himself?" The visitor apologized and said he was leaving, but the bishop ordered him to wait for him in the hall as long as he was already there. After a few moments of what must have been an uncomfortable and nervous silence for the young priest, Eugène commanded Timon-David to enter. In the bishop's quarters, Father Timon-David explained his struggles in his youth apostolate. He felt discouraged and unfit for the task. Suddenly, the grumpy bishop's demeanor warmed, and his irritation vanished. "But my dear child, when you are in trouble, why not come and tell me?" he said. "Am I not your father?" Then, Eugène de Mazenod hugged him, and, while in that embrace, the young priest felt the tears of the bishop flowing onto his cheek. "In those moments, you felt you were ready to lay down your life for him," Timon-David later wrote.

While he cared for all children of God, Eugène had a special attachment to anyone who reciprocated his love for them. Of this characteristic, he wrote, "I admit that I have the weakness of loving better those who know how to communicate to me that I am dear to them. I do not believe that I am too demanding in wanting people to let me know by external expressions the opinion they have of me and what are their feelings in my regard." Decades after writing the above statement, Eugène echoed the same sentiment, "I love with genuine, sincere, tender affection all those who love me. I am sorry for and mourn the loss of all those who are devoted to me or who are devoted to our people or to our holy work. I abhor the selfish, unfeeling hearts that center everything on themselves and give nothing in return for what others give them."

So passionately did Saint Eugène love that he often had to check himself to make sure he was not loving people in such a manner as to take away from loving the One who created them. In 1839, he wrote:

> I had overreached my limits in the love that, from my tender years, I had entertained for my peers, that I had especially overreached those limits in my claim of meriting in return the same expression of love from those to whom I wished

so much good that my heart seemed to lay claim to be loved even more as they responded to my love. No matter what my deluded reason might say, this right belongs only to God. No matter what claims it might have alleged to demand the gratitude of men, it was mistaken.

Passion and Determination

Saint Eugène de Mazenod's struggle to control his love for others was symptomatic of his entire personality. He grew up in Provence, a region in the southern portion of France that was home to a group of people known for their fiery and passionate personalities, and the young Eugène de Mazenod was no exception, as was the rest of his family. When he undertook a task or project, he was unable to produce anything less than his full efforts. Eugène's tutor during his time in Venice told him, "Your character will not allow you to do things halfway. You will do much harm or much good."

Eugène was a man of extremes. He was quick to anger but would always be overcome with guilt if his anger caused him to hurt someone else. One of the first to give an account of the life of Saint Eugène de Mazenod, Bishop Jacques Jeancard said, "I also saw the Superior General explode in righteous anger with an overwhelming power; and then, with a charity no less ardent, to apply himself in a most merciful and consoling way to humility and repentance." However, if someone corrected his wrongdoings with arrogance, he would not admit to the wrong. On the other hand, if he was corrected prudently, he would not say one word to defend his actions. Taming this dual-natured personality would be a lifelong struggle for Eugène.

This passionate and uncompromising attitude also proved to be quite beneficial when it came to founding the Missionary Oblates of Mary Immaculate and leading the Diocese of Marseilles. Eugène would not flinch in the face of opposition. To describe that aspect of his personality, he wrote:

When the malice of men, aided and abetted by all the most devilish of the fiends of Hell, succeeds in thwarting my plans by upsetting everything around me, I then take measures to uncover in my character some resources against misfortune. And far from disheartening me, by a special grace of God, my resources redouble and the energy of my spirit grows in proportion to the peril. It seems that I replenish my strength from the lost courage of those who surround me or whom I meet on my way.

In the process of establishing and receiving approval for a missionary society, Saint Eugène de Mazenod faced opposition from many within the Church. His boldness and courage helped sustain his organization, even when all seemed bleak.

Yet, it must also be noted that Eugène did not choose to face obstacles and start ambitious projects of his own volition. He reported in an 1835 letter to his best friend:

People are always making rash judgments. Because in my lifetime I have successfully managed some difficult situations that would perhaps have been too much for most people, they think that I am enterprising by nature and have a need for activity and to be busy. The truth is quite the contrary. If I have been an active man, if I have led a busy life, if I have undertaken difficult enterprises and brought them to a happy conclusion, it is because of a sense of duty, it was because it was impossible for me not to face the facts that indicated to me that such was the mission that Providence was giving me; whereas on the basis of my temperament I have always had a strong aversion to all kinds of public affairs.

The many actions and projects Saint Eugène de Mazenod undertook were the direct result of his obedience to the will of God. He preferred to be in the background. In several instances,

Eugène journaled about his desire to live a monastic life, but he never acted upon those impulses because he knew the Lord had other plans for him. When he did take action, though, he gave his all.

Eugène de Mazenod would not do anything half-way. This all-or-nothing personality would affect his spiritual life in a unique way. On one occasion, he had an opportunity to pray before the relics of Saint Serenus. Those who were with him reported that he laid prostrate before the reliquary and wept for over fifteen minutes.

Admiration of Virtue and Disgust of Vice

Eugène looked to the saints not so much for their intercession as an example of a virtuous life. He admired Saint Aloysius Gonzaga's chastity and practices of mortification. When it came to evangelization and living an apostolic life, Eugène took Saint Ignatius of Loyola as his example. He also had a special devotion to the Blessed Virgin Mary (see Chapter XXV), his patron Saint Charles, and his guardian angel.

Eugène also strove to imitate the virtue he saw in others on earth, if possible. When he saw virtue in those around him, Eugène became inspired to elevate his own virtuous practices, but when virtue was absent in those with whom he associated, his virtuous habits diminished. Eugène reported that it was difficult for him to be impressed by others:

> I am so little inclined to let myself be impressed by others that I tend to the opposite extreme and frequently have to force myself to pause for reflection to maintain a just balance; it is an undeniable fact and if I sin it is much more through a natural tendency to bend others to my views. Such is the judgment I am constrained to make on myself, such is the judgment of everyone who has known me.

Furthermore, Eugène despised lifestyles that were absent of God. While immersed in the aristocratic social scenes in Palermo and Aix, he felt empty. He abhorred the vanity he saw around him and the flattery that encouraged it. Eugène tried to avoid such behavior. "I have always been exceptionally frank, and this makes me steer clear of using any kind of flattering compliments that would in any way at all call my sincerity into question," he wrote of such behavior. Moreover, the attitudes of the elite social class led to jealousy which he also detested. "I hate jealousy and regard it as a vice unworthy of a generous heart," he wrote.

II

Into Exile

Storms on the Horizon

French society was split into three tiers (called estates): the nobility, the clergy, and everyone else. The power rested with the first two tiers, even though the third tier vastly outnumbered the other two tiers combined. Food became scarce, and the people did not have the political power to make the changes necessary to make food more available to all classes. Meanwhile, the government was in dire need of money. To raise the necessary funds to perpetuate the status quo, taxes were raised on the commoners. This displeased the third estate because those with actual wealth and power—the nobility and the clergy—were exempted from taxes. Unrest began brewing, and in 1789, the animosity towards the current social order hit a boiling point. The people stormed Bastille Prison on July 14, and the French Revolution was officially underway. Revolutionary ideas began spreading throughout France, and in 1790, they caused tensions to explode in Provence.

Eight-year-old Eugène de Mazenod had some sense that something was happening in the world around him, but at his young age, he could not fully comprehend it. He witnessed the worried looks of his parents and noticed the higher frequency with which visitors came to the house, speaking in hushed tones. But, his parents would not have given him a full explanation of the situation.

Eugène's father, Charles-Antoine de Mazenod, president of the Court of Accounts in Aix, was directly affected by the ideas promoted by the revolutionists. Ever the statesman, Charles-Antoine sought to end the crisis and began a campaign to defend the rights of the nobility. Citing precedent and the law, he wrote and made many pleas for an end to the uprisings. His efforts to ease the tensions had no chance of succeeding. Due to the proletariat's disdain for tradition and the current government, any appeals to the rules of the Ancien Regime were destined to be ignored. It was a new age, and when Charles-Antoine clung to the old regime, he became a marked man.

Fear in the de Mazenod home heightened when rioting began in Aix. Charles-Antoine knew he needed to take precautions. On December 12, a disturbance broke out near the Cours Mirabeau. Two days later another riot ended with the lynching of two noblemen. From his bedroom window that overlooked the lamppost where the two men were hung, Eugène could see the corpses, probably frightened and grateful that his father had snuck out of town the day before. Dressed as a hunter, Charles-Antoine de Mazenod snuck into the forest and then out of town just as the people began searching for him, or rather, for his head.

To Nice

Initially, just Charles-Antoine and his brother[2] traveled to Nice (part of the Kingdom of the Piedmont at this point in history) to wait for the Revolution to fizzle out and die. However, they began hearing whispers that the sons of noblemen were under threat. Charles-Antoine also had concerns not only over what the revolutionaries might to do his son, but also

---

[2] Charles-Louis-Eugène de Mazenod, known within the family mostly as "Le Chevalier" and occasionally as "Uncle Eugène" in letters from Marie-Rose to Eugène, was a former commander in the French navy who had fought in the American Revolution.

over Eugène's teachers who were eschewing the traditions of the Catholic Faith in favor of the ideals of the Revolution. Knowing he needed to take action, he sent his brother to Aix with orders to retrieve Eugène and bring him to Nice.

Eugène's mother did not expect her husband to take her son away from her. It was now January 1791, and tensions had calmed down considerably since December. Marie-Rose de Mazenod was hesitant to let her brother-in-law take her son to Nice, but after a family meeting, she consented to the plan.

Eugène's ever-sensitive heart could not bear to leave without saying farewell to a family with whom he was close. During this conversation, Eugène did a remarkable job keeping his emotions under control, excusing himself just before his tears began to flow. With that, Eugène left France for Nice and would not return to his native country for over eleven years.

Early Exile

Nice

From January to April of 1791, Saint Eugène de Mazenod was alone with his father and uncle in Nice, separated from the rest of his family. For the first time in his life, Eugène experienced loneliness. He was a child living with two adults and had left his sister and all his friends behind in France. At the school he attended, he was lost. Classes were taught in Italian, a language Eugène did not speak. In order to complete his assignments, he was forced to stop strangers in the street to help him understand what he was reading.

When conditions in France necessitated it, Charles-Antoine summoned his wife and daughter to join him in exile, and Eugène was overjoyed to be reunited with them. He was also pleased to see that his grandmother Catherine Élisabeth (née Bonnet) Joannis, aunt Élisabeth Gabrielle Alexandrine Dedons de Pierrefeu, and cousin Émile Dedons de Pierrefeu accompanied his mother and sister.

The joy Eugène felt upon seeing his grandmother Joannis was not shared by his father, however. In a letter to a friend, Charles-Antoine de Mazenod wrote, "My wife alone with me and my wife surrounded by her family members are two very different people. The first is an angel. I do not know what name to give the second." As soon as they arrived in Nice, Madame Joannis and her two daughters gained complete control over family affairs. Charles-Antoine and Le Chevalier had no say in any of the decisions. If they objected to anything, the Joannis women would rise up against them in a manner Charles-Antoine likened to "some kind of Furies." The de Mazenod men resigned themselves to simply giving into their demands. Charles-Antoine described their three-pronged strategy for dealing with the Joannis women as "gentleness, patience, and retreat to our room."

After four months in Nice, Madame Joannis was called home by her husband, and tensions between the two families dissipated. Marie-Rose completely changed once her mother left, becoming more patient and pleasant. Charles-Antoine also succeeded in winning over Marie-Rose's sister, who also became more peaceful.

To Turin

Charles-Antoine de Mazenod expected the rioting and disturbances in his home country to last for a brief period of time followed by a restoration of the Ancien Regime. However, it soon became apparent that this would not occur and that he should prepare for a longer period of exile than he had anticipated. This meant arranging for the best education possible for his young son.

The school Eugène de Mazenod attended in Nice provided a better education than the scandalous teachers[3] who had taught him in Aix-en-Provence, but Charles-Antoine knew he could find a better education for his son. Using his connections

---

[3] In Aix, Saint Eugène de Mazenod had been educated at the Collège Bourbon, the same school his father had attended. When Charles-Antoine de Mazenod and his brothers attended that school, the staff was made up of Jesuits. However, the Jesuits had been suppressed, and the Doctrinaires took over management of the school. In 1791, the Doctrinaires accepted the anti-religious code of the Civil Constitution of Clergy, which had been condemned by Pope Pius VI.

within the world of European nobles and royalty, he arranged to have his son accepted into the College of Nobles in Turin, a more prestigious school than the previous schools Eugène had attended. Charles-Antoine and his family accompanied the boy to his new school in September of 1791, but they did not take up residence with him.

In addition to academic reasons, Charles-Antoine and Marie-Rose de Mazenod had another motivation for sending their son to Turin. A growth had formed on Eugène's face and was beginning to disfigure him. If Eugène was in Turin, his parents could use their connections to get the personal physician of King Victor-Amadeus III to remove the growth.

Charles-Antoine and Marie-Rose planned to be present for the surgery. Wishing to spare his parents any anguish they might feel while watching him have the operation, Eugène spoke with the staff at his school to reschedule the procedure so it would be finished before his parents arrived. The staff consented, and the doctor came to the school to remove the growth. When Eugène saw the doctor's instruments, fear overtook him, and he decided to wait for his parents. However, overcome by shame and disappointment in himself, he prayed to God for courage when he returned to his room. His prayer was granted, and he rushed out to have the staff call the doctor back to the school.

Eugène endured the surgery without anesthesia which was not yet available for surgical procedures. The young patient did not once cry out in pain during the ten-minute procedure, despite feeling every incision. The doctor admired his courage, and his parents were relieved that Eugène's calm demeanor helped make the surgery a success.

Eugène's Life in Turin

Eugène excelled at the College of Nobles. He had struggled with the Italian language while in Nice, but during his time in Turin, he was able to master the language and perform well in school. Historical documents reveal the high marks he received in his classes and the words of praise his instructors showered on him. Eugène impressed the Barnabites who taught him not only by his academic efforts, but also in his personal conduct.[4] He showed respect to his teachers and fellow students, followed the rules, and displayed great bravery during the medical procedure he underwent while at the College of Nobles.

Furthermore, Eugène celebrated two spiritual milestones while in Turin. On April 5, 1792, Eugène received First Holy Communion on Holy Thursday, the day the Church remembers the institution of the Eucharist. A few weeks later, on the Feast of the Holy Trinity, June 3, 1792, he received the Sacrament of Confirmation in the chapel of Turin's archbishop, Cardinal Costa.

The Family Joins Eugène in Turin

Charles-Antoine had desired to live near his son in Turin, but his wife did not agree to leave Nice. Marie-Rose could receive mail from her mother three times per week there; whereas, if they moved to Turin, she would only receive mail from her mother twice per week. Not wanting to give the Joannis family another reason to dislike him, Charles-Antoine acquiesced to his wife's desires and accepted the separation from his son, a decision he would soon regret.

The famine that helped spark the French Revolution now began to inspire war. The new ruling powers in France decided the solution to the famine was to invade other countries and pillage their food supply. As the French army began advancing, the lives of émigrés (those who had fled France as a result of the French Revolution) once again fell into peril. The de Mazenod

---

[4] Eugène's conduct was not without flaw, however. As a twenty-four year old, he stated in a letter to a friend that he still had "pleasurable memories of the punches that I rained on the fat cheeks of those Piedmontese classmates of ours, to protect you against their harassment."

family had a chance to take their possessions with them to Turin and be near their son, but they chose to stay where they were. Nice was one of the first cities to fall, and the de Mazenods were forced to abandon most of their possessions[5] as they fled just two months after they had dropped their son off at the College of Nobles. The loss of property plunged the de Mazenod family into poverty.

Upon their arrival in Turin, the de Mazenod family faced uncertainty with regards to their safety and security. All Frenchmen had been ordered to leave Turin. Relying upon his connections to the Prime Minister, Charles-Antoine de Mazenod arranged for an exception, allowing them to stay. The family settled in a town outside Turin and battled the cold of winter while struggling to scrape enough money to appear as though they were living as lavishly as was to be expected of a noble family.

The family's financial strains increased when they were joined by two more family members, Charles-Antoine's brother, Fortuné, vicar general of Aix, and uncle, Charles-Auguste-André, who held the same position in Marseilles. Both Fathers de Mazenod had remained in France until August 1792 to carry out their priestly duties,[6] despite the peril they faced.[7] They fled to Switzerland first before joining the rest of the family in Turin.

---

[5] Marie-Rose left Nice two days before Charles-Antoine and his brother Le Chevalier, but she refused to bring eleven trunks of their possessions with her because she found the fee to transport them to be too expensive. When the brothers de Mazenod were forced to flee, they could only bring the clothes they were wearing.

[6] The archbishop and other vicars general of Aix had fled at the outset of the French Revolution, leaving Fortuné to administer the Archdiocese of Aix alone.

[7] Fortuné de Mazenod had been fired upon during a Eucharistic procession on the Feast of Corpus Christi in 1791.

The Beginnings of a Nomadic Lifestyle

Even in Italy, the Revolution was a source of anguish and fear. Eugène's academic success and the graces that flowed from his reception of the final two Sacraments of Initiation were to be overshadowed by the danger creeping towards them. In April of 1794, the armies of the new regime in France were moving towards Turin and began threatening their adopted city. The decision was made to flee again. Upon the suggestion of a friend of Charles-Antoine, the family chose to move to Venice which would prove to be an excellent choice given the effect living in Venice would have on young Eugène. "It was during that time that a true man of God struck the foundations of faith and piety in my soul, which he had prepared beforehand by his skillful direction, aided by the Holy Spirit whose instrument he was," he later wrote. "And upon these same foundations did God, in His mercy, build the edifice of my spiritual life."

Don Bartolo Zinelli

Arrival in Venice

When they arrived in Venice, the de Mazenod family was disappointed to discover that the town was crowded due to the Feast of the Ascension, and there was nowhere to stay, forcing them to sleep two more nights on the boat that had brought them to Venice. A fellow traveler, who had conned his way onto their boat, helped them find two rooms in the home of a tavern-keeper. The family and their servants, a total of eleven people, crammed themselves into those rooms for a month until a more permanent dwelling could be found.

Once the visitors to the city left, Eugène's father found a place for the family to live, and Charles-Antoine could not have chosen a better location for his family's dwelling, for the window at which Eugène used to sit and daydream was located directly across from the home of the Zinelli family, who would be very influential in the young Frenchman's life.

A Tutor for Eugène

Monsignor Milesi, pastor of the church of Saint Sylvester in Venice, could not help but notice and wonder about Eugène de Mazenod who served Mass for his uncle and granduncle every day. He knew the sorry state of the family's finances made it impossible to send Eugène to a proper school, and he also knew the dangers a twelve-year-old boy could encounter if left to his own devices in the city of Venice.⁸ A plan began to form in his head to provide this young boy with someone to educate him and to help him grow in holiness.

Milesi knew the perfect man for the job—Don Bartolo Zinelli. This young priest lived with his family in Venice and spent his days studying while waiting for the Jesuit order, which had been suppressed by a papal bull in 1773, to be restored. The pastor of Saint Sylvester knew the virtue of Don Bartolo and his family. He also knew that this holy, young priest lived near the residence of the French émigrés. Zinelli was not only a virtuous tutor, but a convenient one as well.

Knowing that, as they move from childhood into adolescence, boys often develop a rebellious streak, Milesi and Zinelli took steps to ensure the boy did not feel as though a tutor was being forced upon him. They secretly summoned Charles-Antoine and Marie-Rose de Mazenod and divulged their plan to them. With their consent, they set their plan in motion.

One day, as Eugène sat at his window daydreaming, Don Bartolo appeared at the window across from him. He got his attention and asked him if he was worried about wasting his day sitting there daydreaming. The boy responded by telling the young priest that he was a foreigner with no books, nor the money to buy any or to hire a tutor. Don Bartolo offered to loan him a book, and within moments, a book was tossed from one window to the other. The eager, young Frenchman devoured the book, finishing it before the day ended.

The next morning, the boy's parents advised him to return the book. Eugène crossed over to the Zinelli home and was shown to the library. There, Don Bartolo showed him three chairs. The first was where Don Bartolo spent his days studying. His brother, also a priest waiting for the Jesuits to be restored,

---

⁸ In his memoirs, Bishop de Mazenod wrote, "What a republic of dissolute living was the Venice of that time!"

used the second one. The third had been vacant since their brother had passed away. This chair was offered to Eugène who enthusiastically accepted the offer. The deception had worked, and Eugène began to learn from a man about whom he would later write, "But for him, I would never have known God."

This cunning plan would not have come to fruition without Monsignor Milesi. He instigated all that took place and is responsible for bringing the young boy and Don Bartolo Zinelli together. Years later, Eugène would express great gratitude for the influence of Monsignor Milesi on his life:

> My true friend, the former parish priest Milesi, who had been my confessor during my early youth, who showed me such fatherly affection, who so often had seen to my childish needs, in a word, who loved me as if I was his own child, he is the one who in his touching concern for me introduced me to blessed Bartolo Zinelli and gently suggested to him what he had to do to instruct me in the life of prayer and the humanities.

Moral Example

Eugène de Mazenod found in Don Bartolo Zinelli the first real example of moral conduct he had ever witnessed. Other than his uncle and granduncle who were priests, he had no one in his family to whom he could look for an example on how one ought to live. His parents exhibited many character flaws (discussed more in Chapter V). Le Chevalier, Eugène's uncle Eugène, was no saint, only marrying in 1812 to legitimize his relationship with his concubine and died heavily in debt. The maternal side of Eugène's family exhibited volatile and treacherous behavior (discussed more in Chapter V and Chapter IX). The young priest who mentored Eugène not only lived a moral life, but also instructed Eugène on how to do the same. Eugène later wrote, "O blessed Zinelli! What would I have become without you? What thanks do I not owe God for having provided me with the acquaintance and the friendship of such a holy person!"

Life as Don Bartolo's Student

Eugène spent the majority of his time at the Zinelli home. After Mass, the mornings were entirely devoted to lessons. His textbook[9] was designed to provide "young people of either sex adequate ideas on the majority of the fields of human knowledge, morality, history of Religion, mythology, general and particular physics, astronomy, natural history, geography, history of France, etc." At lunch time, he returned home to dine with his family, except on Sundays and Thursdays when he dined with the Zinellis. Following lunch, Don Bartolo and his student went for a walk to one of the churches in Venice to pray. The lessons resumed when they returned to Don Bartolo's home and lasted until the evening.

Eugène spent his evenings at the Zinelli home, as well. The Zinellis were usually joined by some Italian and French priests who would gather to pray evening prayer and to discuss the issues of the day. Listening to their discussions allowed Eugène to learn about the debates over Jansenism and Ultramontanism and where faithful Catholics ought to stand on these matters. Eugène would remain with the Zinellis for supper and night prayer. It was customary in Venice for the evening meal to conclude around midnight, meaning he would arrive home late and see little of his family.

Eugène's parents were too grateful for the opportunities Eugène was receiving to be upset over seeing so little of their son. They were, no doubt, pleased that the financial burden of educating and feeding the boy had been practically eliminated. Eugène, for his part, greatly enjoyed the opportunity to learn and be accepted as a member of the Zinelli family.

---

[9] Jean Jacques Fillassier, *Eraste, ou l'Ami de la jeunesse*.

Life as Don Bartolo's pupil was not easy, however. Apart from the rigorous academic plan, Don Bartolo also gave Eugène strict regulations for his spiritual life that followed the teachings of Saint Ignatius of Loyola. He believed that "[i]n young people, virtue is like a plant that needs to be deeply rooted. Otherwise, it will quickly wither and die. And it must be well protected, well watered, and well nourished." Zinelli's approach to advising Eugène on his spiritual life focused on growing virtue within Eugène and making it habitual.

The rule of life Don Bartolo made his student draw up for himself stated that, after praying a morning prayer on his knees, Eugène would "unite my weak acts of adoration to those of the Sacred Hearts of Jesus and Mary, the Angels and the Saints…I will recite an Our Father slowly and with great respect for this prayer which issued from the lips of our Lord Jesus Christ Himself." Next, Eugène would offer his day to the Lord:

> I offer You my exercises of piety, my studies, my duties, my most ordinary actions…in union with the sentiments of His adorable Heart…You, O Mary, after God my dearest hope, you, my guardian angel, my holy patrons, you, the saints of Heaven, souls of Purgatory, assist me in all my actions; be my advocates before God and the Heart of Jesus.

Young Eugène's morning prayer routine concluded with several more acts of piety. He prayed a "De Profundis for my dear departed." Then, on bended knee, he would face in the direction of a church and pray, "Jesus, Son of David, I will not let You go unless You bless me." Turning towards a picture of Mary he prayed using the words of Saint Stanislaus, "True Mother of the Savior, adoptive mother of the sinner, enfold me in the bosom of your maternal piety." Lastly, Eugène would "take holy water; I will respectfully kiss my crucifix in the area of the wounds of the Heart, the hand of Mary, my mother. Having arranged everything for the greater glory of God, I will leave my room to go about my business." Despite the many steps of this routine, Eugène made sure to limit the total length of this time of prayer to less than fifteen minutes because he did not want to burden himself with "many lengthy practices of piety," preferring to perform small acts of prayer, "but faithfully and with fervor."

Furthermore, under Zinelli's spiritual care, Eugène's daily devotions included serving Mass, praying the Little Office of the Blessed Virgin, fifteen to thirty minutes of spiritual reading, and the Rosary. He went to Confession with Monsignor Milesi every Saturday and would receive Communion every Sunday. Zinelli also taught Eugène Ignatian meditation and instructed him on how to apply those mediations to Scripture and to his situation in life. The spiritual works Eugène read, particularly those of Saint Aloysius Gonzaga, led him to practice mortification. He chose to fast every Friday and three days per week during Lent. Choosing to increase the amount of fasting takes on a special significance for a young, growing boy, especially those who, like Eugène, will grow to be six feet tall[10] by the age of twenty. On Saturdays, he often slept on top of sticks so that he would wake up early to spend as much time in church as possible. The sticks hardly seem necessary considering he chose to sleep on the floor. While these were the general spiritual guidelines he followed, Eugène did follow the advice of Saint Francis de Sales to adapt to whatever various circumstances might demand.

Eugène loved the lifestyle he lived under Zinelli's care, and despite its rigors, embraced it whole heartily. In a diary he kept of his experiences in exile, Eugène wrote:

> Can I ever thank God sufficiently for getting for me, out of His infinite goodness, help such as this precisely at the most

---

[10] Six feet was several inches taller than the average height, for the time period.

difficult time of life, a decisive time for me, in which were planted by a man of God, in my soul prepared by his skillful hand and the grace of the Holy Spirit whose instrument he was, the fundamentals of religion and piety on which the mercy of God has built the edifice of my spiritual life? It was in the school of this holy priest that I learnt to despise worldly vanities, to taste the things of God: far removed from all dissipation, from every contact with young people of my age, I did not even give a thought to what constitutes the object of their desires…I had derived from my pious reading a certain attraction for mortification…My health came to no harm at all from it, and I persevered with this regime for as long as I lived in Venice.

Here Eugène expresses love for a lifestyle most youths of today's society would find abhorrent and unnecessarily uncomfortable, even those who take the Catholic Faith and the practice of mortification seriously. It is a testament to the heroic virtue with which Eugène lived his life, and he justifiably credits his childhood mentors for inspiring him to become holy. They managed to mold a stubborn young boy into a person of great sanctity and did so when Eugène was at an age when most boys rebel. Simply put, without the influence of Milesi and Zinelli, the Church would have never recognized Eugène de Mazenod as a saint.

Catholic Without Embarrassment

The rigorous spiritual plan Don Bartolo assigned to Eugène created courageous virtue in the young Frenchman. In 1795, Eugène attended a dinner party at the Venetian home of the Spanish ambassador to the Most Serene Republic. When it was time for the meal, all approached the table, and Eugène waited to sit down until the meal prayer had been said. However, everyone else sat down without even thinking about a meal prayer. All eyes turned towards Eugène, the only one who was still standing. Unable to shirk his religious duty, this pupil of Don Bartolo Zinelli boldly made the Sign of the Cross and said the meal prayer, without regard for what anyone present would think of him.

A Seed is Planted

"Whatever I am, I owe to Don Bartolo," Saint Eugène would later say of his teacher. "He was a real saint, one worthy of canonization." It was during his stay in Venice and under the tutelage of Don Bartolo Zinelli that the founder of the Missionary Oblates of Mary Immaculate would first feel called to the priesthood.

On a daily basis, Eugène found himself in the presence of Don Bartolo, Monsignor Milesi, his uncle, his granduncle, and often other priests. These men would be an example to him of the priestly life. Eugène felt drawn to live as they did. Bishop Jeancard described the effect these men had on him:

> Since he had before him the example of holy living of his two teachers, since he took part in their conversations, their readings and several of their religious exercises every day, he already felt enkindling within him the all-embracing fervor of a generous piety. Then, at night back in his father's house, he found in the persons of his two venerated uncles, the one grand vicar of Aix and the other of Marseilles, an example of the same kind of edifying life. This strengthened yet more the sentiments he already entertained in his heart…It was at that point that the thought he had been entertaining first manifested itself. He expressed to his parents his resolve to consecrate himself to God in the ecclesiastical state.

Young Eugène had no doubt of his priestly vocation. "I was only twelve years old when God planted in my heart the first real desires to devote my life to the missions," he wrote in 1855. Eugène's holy tutor, not long after the de Mazenods were forced to leave Venice, joined a religious community called the Society of the Priests of the Faith, dedicated to restoring the Society of Jesus. Even before joining this order, Don Bartolo had been praying for the return of the Jesuit order.

This desire to not only restore the Society of Jesus, but to also become one was a desire Zinelli had hoped to pass on to his pupil. Eugène himself would later admit that had he "stayed in Venice a year longer, I would have followed my saintly director and his brother, who had become a priest, into the religious congregation of their choice, where both of them died in the practice of heroic virtue."

When Charles-Auguste-André de Mazenod, former vicar general of Marseilles, heard that his young grandnephew had expressed interest in one day becoming a priest, he, knowing how the fancies of young boys change from day to day, decided to discuss this with the young boy in order to conduct a minor investigation into this potential vocation and to tease his grandnephew a little as well. He asked him if it was true that he wanted to become a priest, and the boy responded emphatically in the affirmative. The elderly priest pointed out to Eugène that he was the only son of a noble family and, if he became a priest, his family name would die out. The response from the young boy floored his granduncle. "What greater honor could come to our family than to have it end with a priest?" he said. Taken aback by this answer, Canon Charles-Auguste-André de Mazenod gave his blessing to the young boy who would later be the bishop of the diocese where he had served as vicar general. Eugène's absolute conviction of his vocation would sadly become muted in the years to come, amid the noise and anguish of his life.

V

A Broken Family

Love of Family

Saint Eugène de Mazenod possessed a deep love for his family. Upon his entrance into Saint Sulpice Seminary in 1808, he described the affection he had for his family to the director of the seminary, "I idolize my family. I would let myself be cut up into little pieces for some members of my family, and that stretches out to quite a long way for I would give my life without hesitation for my father, mother, grandmother, my sister and my father's two brothers." This passionate expression of Eugène's love for his family makes their actions seem especially heartbreaking, for Eugène's family would be the source of great anguish and sadness for him.

Eugène's Mother and Sister Return to France

By 1795, a little over a year into the de Mazenod family's stay in Venice, the Reign of Terror in France had subsided, mitigating many of the dangers facing the émigrés. Recent developments in how their native country was being governed cooled tensions between classes and allowed those who had been bourgeoisie (middle class) prior to their marriage to become bourgeoisie again by divorcing their spouse. By divorcing her husband and returning to her maiden name, Marie-Rose de Mazenod, now Citizen Joannis, could recover the family's assets. She left Venice in October[11] to return to Aix and carry out her plan.

Eugène along with his father accompanied Marie-Rose and Ninette on the return journey as far as Livorno.[12] In this Tuscan city, Eugène said goodbye to his mother and sister, leaving Eugène without any female members of his family. At the time, Eugène did not fully realize what was happening. He felt the full effect of being separated from his mother, but he did not realize it would be seven years before he would see her again.

Picking up His Cross

While in Livorno, Eugène acquired a crucifix to wear around his neck.[13] In Venice, he daily encountered his uncle, his granduncle, Don Bartolo Zinelli, his tutor's brother, and Monsignor Milesi all of whom were priests. If Eugène had wanted a crucifix to wear around his neck, he easily could have received one from one of the many priests he knew. Yet, he chose to acquire one at a time of sorrow. At this point in his life, Eugène had no doubt read the Gospel passage where Jesus says, "If anyone wishes to come after me, he must deny himself and take up his cross daily

---

[11] Joseph Thomas and Catherine Élisabeth Joannis' family had been encouraging their daughters to return to France for a while before either of them did indeed leave exile. Eugène's aunt Élisabeth preceded his mother, leaving Venice in July and taking Eugène's cousin Èmile with her.

[12] Eugène's uncle Fortuné also accompanied Marie-Rose on her return journey. However, he went as far as Switzerland with her because he knew the area, having spent time there prior to joining the family in Turin.

[13] Some staff members at an inn where Eugène's family stopped in Livorno saw the crucifix protruding from underneath the clothing Eugène wore and began to mock him. Instead of removing the sacramental in embarrassment, Eugène shot a look of righteous anger at the men mocking him which immediately silenced them.

and follow me."[14] Eugène knew he needed to embrace the cross of separation from his mother and chose to wear a crucifix to remind himself to unite his sufferings to the suffering of Christ. The act of donning a crucifix at a moment of great hardship is a testament to the strong faith Don Bartolo was instilling in his young pupil, Eugène de Mazenod.

Marie-Rose Saddened by the Separation

In her letters to Eugène, Marie-Rose de Mazenod expressed the pain she felt as a result of leaving the family. "My leaving you," she wrote, "was at the price of great sorrow and a profound grief, my loving and dear child." Leaving her only son was hard for Marie-Rose, but she did so for the good of the family. Eugène's mother was also saddened to be separated from Charles-Antoine de Mazenod, her husband and Eugène's "kind father." "Hug warmly your dear father on my behalf," she said in a letter to Eugène. "Tell him how distressed I am at being separated from him." Her sadness over being separated from her husband would soon dissipate after reuniting with her mother and cousin.

Marie-Rose and the Joannis Family

The marriage contract that arranged the marriage of Charles-Antoine de Mazenod and Marie-Rose Joannis stipulated that the dowry was to remain in Marie-Rose's name, a clause that proved to be beneficial to her. Through her divorce and the business acumen of her mother and cousin, Roze Joannis, Citizen Joannis gained control over almost all of her ex-husband's property and the inheritance due to him following the death of his father, Charles-Alexandre de Mazenod.

Charles-Antoine de Mazenod found the relationship between Marie-Rose and Roze Joannis particularly troubling. They were close, perhaps too close. Charles-Antoine became

---

[14] Luke 9:23.

concerned because of how manipulative he was and because he subscribed to heretical beliefs.[15] Roze also read every letter Charles-Antoine wrote to Marie-Rose and helped her write her responses which were often filled with exaggerations, especially with regards to her health.[16] He became even more concerned when Marie-Rose and Roze went on a three-month vacation to Paris and Vichy. When Charles-Antoine expressed his suspicion of a potential affair between the two, Eugène responded by describing Roze's appearance as a "veritable mass of decrepitude."[17] Yet, he must have had some attractive qualities, for it is known that he fathered at least one illegitimate child. Despite this, there is no historical proof that there was anything more than a close friendship between Marie-Rose and Roze.

Marie-Rose, her mother, and Roze Joannis cannot be blamed for taking control of the de Mazenod family's assets. Doing so greatly assisted the process of ensuring financial security for Eugène and his sister. However, their attitudes towards

---

[15] Roze Joannis was a staunch Jansenist (although, he did criticize anyone who separated himself from the Church). His influence with Marie-Rose diminished the frequency with which she received the Sacraments, something Eugène would later advise against. When he returned to France, Eugène engaged in frequent, theological debates with Roze, especially with regards to the troublesome issues of Jansenism and the frequency with which one should receive the Sacraments. However, towards the end of his life, Roze experienced a conversion which Eugène helped facilitate. His tombstone reads: "Of sound mind, he recanted from his errors…He died happily in the bosom of the Catholic Church."

[16] These exaggerations worried Charles-Antoine until he received letters from friends in France who reported a different description of Marie-Rose's health.

[17] Charles-Antoine, too, criticized Roze's appearance stating, "[A] painter would only have to accurately reproduce his features to have the most faithful image of envy."

the de Mazenod brothers, especially after they had gained control over their assets and began reminding them often that they no longer mattered, make the motivations for their actions seem questionable. After all, they had done the same with Marie-Rose's sister Élisabeth and her husband, the Marquis Dedons de Pierrefeu. He, too, would be left with no assets and would be permanently separated from his wife.

Permanence

During this period in history, many couples went through faux-divorces in order to secure their property, and that was the original intention for the de Mazenods. Marie-Rose did not intend to break a religious vow when she appeared before the local government and requested that her marriage be dissolved. For years following their divorce, both Charles-Antoine and Marie-Rose expressed fondness and love for each other in their letters to one another. However, the romantic sentiments they expressed faded over time.

At times, Eugène's mother, Marie-Rose, appears cold and unloving towards Charles-Antoine and their son Eugène in her letters to them. Yet, her letters do reveal she loved them both, but she also appears to have had a short temper, often agitated by her ever-fluctuating health, causing some friction within the family. Further aggravating the situation was how susceptible Marie-Rose was to her family's influence. Her mother, Èlisabeth Joannis, had a particular distaste for Charles-Antoine.[18] It is, no

---

[18] Part of the animosity Charles-Antoine de Mazenod received from his mother-in-law was due to Madame Joannis' awareness that he had engaged in some flirtations. Charles-Antoine remained loving and attentive to his wife during the time the flirtations took place, admitted he was wrong to engage in them, sought forgiveness from his wife, and asked for his mother-in-law's help in winning back the affection of his wife. Madame Joannis agreed to assist her son-in-law in his efforts to reassure Marie-Rose of his love for

doubt, due to her influence over her daughter that Marie-Rose offered little help towards finding a way for Charles-Antoine to return to France for a marital reunion.[19]

Once Marie-Rose had control over her husband's property, her mother and cousin began to influence her opinion of her husband. Their whispers about him caused her to view Charles-Antoine as unimportant, and he was unable to defend himself in person. Citizen Joannis had his money and his daughter, and in 1802, she would separate him from his son Eugène. Shortly thereafter, she wrote a letter to Charles-Antoine declaring, "You now have nothing." Those words made it clear. The divorce was no longer a piece of paper; Eugène's parents were to be forever separated.[20] Getting a divorce had been an attempt to financially benefit Eugène and Ninette, but it would cause major damage to their morale.

Caught in the Middle

During the time when his parents' fighting was at its most intense point, Eugène was aware of all that was being said

---

her, but did the exact opposite. As this was occurring, the French Revolution began, plunging the family into a deeper crisis and causing a separation between Madame Joannis and her daughter for which she probably blamed Charles-Antoine, not those who threatened to kill or otherwise harm him, her daughter, and her grandchildren.

[19] When amnesty was declared and émigrés were allowed to return to France, Marie-Rose stated that she would not be separated from her mother and that, if Charles-Antoine were to return, he would be forced to live at their country residence in Saint-Laurent to avoid his debtors and because Madame Joannis refused to allow the brothers de Mazenod to live in her home, even if they paid rent. She also refused to help him pay off his debts.

[20] Marie-Rose made this clear to Charles-Antoine by writing to him that he would not see her or Ninette again until Judgement Day.

between the two. Charles-Antoine believed Eugène's prudence was far greater than most boys his age. He, therefore, revealed everything regarding his relationship with Marie-Rose to his son. Knowledge of this must have wounded Eugène's sensitive heart. Throughout his life, Saint Eugène never shied away from expressing his emotions, yet nothing is known of his grief over his parents' divorce. If Eugène could not bring himself to discuss this pain, it must have been profound.

Eugène knew that both the de Mazenod brothers and the Joannis family loved him. Yet, their shared love of him did not bring the two families together. Instead, it drove them further apart. They argued over who should raise him and how he ought to be raised. Eugène was caught in the middle of the battle between the Joannis and de Mazenod families. He did not do anything to cause them to argue, yet he was the reason they were arguing.

Deaths in the Family

While dealing with the separation from his mother and sister as well as his parents' divorce, Eugène was also forced to cope with the loss of three family members. As previously mentioned, his paternal grandfather, Charles-Alexandre de Mazenod,[21] passed away on May 9, 1795. On November 9, his maternal grandfather, Joseph Thomas Joannis, died. Two weeks later, his granduncle, Charles-Auguste-André, died as well, marking the final tragedy in a difficult year for the young Eugène de Mazenod.

---

[21] Eugène's paternal grandfather did not die a peaceful death. He was not skilled with money and incurred large amounts of debt. The debt combined with the French Revolution inspiring disobedient and disrespectful behavior from his servants and a gradual descent into blindness created an unhappy environment for his final days. He died without any sight and without any loved ones near him.

To make matters worse, the task of arranging the funeral for his granduncle fell to Eugène.[22] Fortunately for Eugène, Monsignor Milesi took it upon himself to take care of all the arrangements. The pastor decided against honoring Eugène's request that the funeral expenses be kept to a minimum. Upon seeing what Milesi had done for his granduncle, Eugène was worried about what it would cost, but the good priest assured Eugène that the death of Charles-Auguste-André, who had celebrated Mass in his parish every day, was a loss he felt too and that the costs of the funeral would be taken care of by the parish.

The loss of his granduncle whittled those in exile with him down to his father and two uncles. The older de Mazenod men spent almost all of their time trying to keep the family afloat, leaving Eugène without guidance from them. It is fortunate that he had Don Bartolo and the Zinelli family to be with him during this difficult time. However, the assistance the Zinelli family was able to offer would have most likely been insufficient, for divorce was not as common then as it is now. They would have been unfamiliar with how to help a young man cope with such a tragic set of circumstances.

---

[22] His father and uncles were busy with their business. Not only was their business struggling to survive, but they also had to deal with business partners who acted in their own self-interest and cheated them.

VI

Separation From Don Bartolo

Napoleon Conquers Venice

In 1797, French troops began advancing towards Venice. Most of the French émigrés fled, fearing both Napoleon Bonaparte's army and the Venetians who began to view them as a threat, but Charles-Antoine de Mazenod felt he could not abandon his business partners. His company had fallen on hard times, and leaving immediately, without making arrangements, would have been wrong. Therefore, the de Mazenods resolved to remain in Venice until they had no other option, allowing the young Eugène de Mazenod to witness the fall of Venice to the French army.[23] The de Mazenods, through the intercession of influential friends, were able to avoid the deportation most of their countrymen faced following the French invasion.

Attempt to Return to France

On July 30, 1797, Eugène's mother Marie-Rose made a petition to have her son's name removed from the list of émigrés. Two years prior, a law had been passed stating that no child who had been removed from the country for educational or commercial purposes could be considered an émigré. Her request

---

[23] Eugène would later write of the fall of Venice with disgust, claiming "the Venetians should have shown some backbone instead of running out with open arms to welcome their shame and destruction."

was accepted and Eugène's name was provisionally removed from the list.

However, Eugène's father, former president of the Court of Accounts and Finances of Aix and loyal supporter of the king, faced an uphill battle in getting his name removed from the same list. He invoked a clause of the same law that Marie-Rose had invoked on Eugène's behalf. This clause stated that those who had left France of their own accord to practice their trade were not émigrés. Nine Venetian merchants signed an affidavit stating Charles-Antoine de Mazenod had indeed practiced business in Venice, and it was upon those signatures that he made a petition for removal from the list of émigrés.

At first, the de Mazenod men's plan to return to France looked like it might succeed. The political volatility had cooled. By the end of July 1797, many Provençal émigrés had already returned safely to France, including Eugène's uncle Fortuné. Charles-Antoine felt a great need to return to France. He resented the control Marie-Rose's mother and cousin had over her. Fortuné had been sent with instructions to take care of his affairs in France, but Charles-Antoine feared his brother would not possess the firmness needed to work with his mother-in-law. However, plans for returning to France were halted in August when the political climate took a turn for the worse, forcing the de Mazenods to extend their exile.

The Need to Leave Venice

Following the entrance of French soldiers into Venice, local sentiment towards Frenchmen, even the émigrés who also despised the army of revolutionary France, became hostile. Matters worsened for the de Mazenods when the admiral of the French navy visited their home. The Admiral knew Eugène's uncle Charles-Louis-Eugène from the latter's time serving in the King's Navy and went to see his old comrade. This visit soured the de Mazenods' reputation in Venice, but endeared them to the members of the French military occupying the city. In his memoirs, Saint Eugène wrote:

> We were then looked upon as a family that was suspect and it took the whole weight of the good opinion people had developed over a period of four years associating with the honorable gentlemen that my father and my uncles were to dispel the negative impression of the admiral's visit which was wholly out of friendship and certainly without political motivation.

Charles-Antoine knew that if the French soldiers left, they would no longer be protected from the people of Venice. A strange twist of fate had occurred. The de Mazenods had been fleeing the French army, but now they were being protected by it. However, plans did need to be made in the event an exodus became necessary. Charles-Antoine and his brother made arrangements for the liquidation of the remaining merchandise from their business, and after being unable to obtain a passport to Germany, the de Mazenods chose Naples as their next exilian home.

Leaving Don Bartolo

When they felt it was no longer safe to remain in Venice, Charles-Antoine, his brothers, and his son Eugène left, bound for Naples, on November 11, 1797. Leaving Venice meant leaving Eugène's tutor Don Bartolo and his surrogate family. Don Bartolo had been an excellent teacher, a close friend, and his watchful protector in Venice, and this separation was a moment of intense pain for Eugène. Sadly, this desolation was only a foreshadowing of what was yet to come.

During Eugène's time in Venice, he and Don Bartolo saw their relationship as more than just that of a student and a teacher; they were friends. When Eugène and his family left for

Livorno, Don Bartolo wrote Eugène a letter expressing sentiments of a close friendship:

> Your letter so filled with sentiments of affection and heartfelt friendship infinitely beyond what I deserve, I cannot tell you what it stirred up in my heart in terms of gratitude, tenderness along with bitterness and pain. What a harsh fate separated me so unexpectedly from the one I love with such a sincere affection, from a young man with such an upright heart with such great hopes, from you, most dear and loved Master Eugène, a separation which took place without giving me the opportunity of seeing you again for one moment to give you a warm embrace!...It was God's will! I could only close my eyes and submit myself to His sovereign designs. But what a sacrifice for my heart? It has led me to this reflection: If friendship is so sweet on earth, how incomparably more sweet will it be in Heaven! Oh, if Divine Mercy leads us there, then what full and perfect happiness for our friendship! Let us do everything in our power, dear Eugene, to become worthy of this good fortune.
>
> After all, the world is only perpetual change, a giddy whirlwind, a measureless abyss. Woe betide the person who casts himself into it. *Sortitus es animam bonam.* (You were endowed with a good soul.) I pray God will keep it so for you and that He will increase in you those sentiments of piety and holy fear with which He has endowed you, to guard you during those years when the passions rear their heads, that He may lead you to taste the pure delights of being in his service and of despising the seductions of the world, finally, not only that He bless you *de rore coeli,* (with the dew of heaven) but also *de pinguedine terrae* (from the fertility of the earth).

In Venice, Eugène received his first real taste of friendship. It would not be until he felt supreme loneliness in Naples and Palermo, however, that he would realize what he had in Venice. His desire for virtuous friendship would go unsatisfied for almost a decade.

To Naples

Due to their poor financial health, the de Mazenods could only afford to travel via a cattle boat. Difficult winds, the health of their captain, the threat of pirate attacks, and other misfortunes made the journey long and difficult, but after fifty-one days, they arrived in Naples on January 1, 1798. Shortly thereafter, they were reunited with Eugène's uncle Father Fortuné de Mazenod, who was compelled to leave France again just weeks after his return to his native country.

The Location of Eugène's Mother

When Fortuné reunited with his family in Naples, he unfortunately brought no news of the whereabouts of Eugène's mother. She too had to leave France again, but did not tell her son or husband where she went. Charles-Antoine and Eugène had heard nothing from Marie-Rose and were worried.

Historical records show she and her cousin had obtained passports for Spain and Switzerland in September of 1797. This may have been a rouse, however, as there is evidence she was living somewhere in France in August of 1798. Regardless of where she was, Marie-Rose did not join her husband and son in exile, nor did she reveal her location to them.

The secrecy irked Charles-Antoine. The anguish he felt may have been symptomatic of the larger dispute between Charles-Antoine and Marie-Rose. If he had wanted to find a logical reason for not learning of his wife's location, he could have found one, for there were reasons why Charles-Antoine never heard from Marie-Rose. The lack of word may have been due to the deplorable state of the mail service or the paranoia within the French government who frequently searched the mail and confiscated letters they did not wish to be sent. Nevertheless, the lack of news and Charles-Antoine's resulting bitterness further widened the chasm of the couple's emotional separation.

Financial Struggles

While in Naples, the de Mazenods' financial position weakened even more. Charles-Antoine and his business partners' company went bankrupt, and the de Mazenod family arrived in Naples with only enough money to last seven months. Luckily, due to Charles-Antoine's political connections, he was able to secure an allowance from the Queen of Naples. Marie-Rose de Mazenod, on the other hand, offered little financial help to her husband, son, and brothers-in-law, and due to the conditions she placed on the stipend and his pride, Charles-Antoine refused to accept even that. In order to save money, the de Mazenod men ate only a "dish of bitter and detestable boiled quince" for their evening meal.[24]

Overwhelming Monotony of the Saddest Kind

The sorry state of the de Mazenods' finances meant Eugène's education suffered. He was able to study German under a tutor for three months and learned much in that time, but, after three months, his teacher died, as did Eugène's knowledge of the language. His father and uncles were too busy managing their finances to have the necessary time to tutor Eugène and were unable to hire another teacher.

Eugène had nothing to do except sit at home, leaving only to go to the church to serve Mass for his uncle and to go with his father to visit the elder de Mazenod's friends. He had been in this situation before. Just as he was when he first arrived in Venice, the young man was in a new home in a new city. Yet,

---

[24] Charles-Antoine de Mazenod in a letter to the Baron of Talleyrand dated October 19, 1802.

he was not filled with the excitement moving to a new city can bring. Instead, he was filled with despair. Naples held no new opportunities for the fifteen-year-old Frenchman. All he could do was sit in his home, alone with his thoughts, for every second of every day. Unfortunately, there would be no Don Bartolo Zinelli to call out to him as he sat by a window to invite him into a holy home that helped mold him and nurture a priestly vocation. "My stay in Naples was a year of overwhelming monotony of the saddest kind for me," Eugène later wrote. "I no longer had my good friends, the Zinellis, near me, nor did I have any daily occupation or association suited to my tastes and inclinations. I readily admit that my time was wasted, but I don't think it was my fault."

Fortunately, Eugène was able to correspond with Don Bartolo who tried as best he could to advise him from afar. The advice he gave to Eugène was to keep up his spiritual practices, overcome any obstacles to continuing his education, and find good friends. Don Bartolo's advice was impossible to accomplish. Eugène was able to get to Confession weekly (although, his confessor was unable to provide the quality of advice Eugène received from Zinelli and Milesi in Venice) and to receive Communion every Sunday, but he was unable to find any materials for spiritual reading. Eugène tried to explain this to his former tutor, but Don Bartolo did not understand the full extent of his former pupil's predicament. Despite the lack of resources to aid his spiritual development, Eugène's moral conduct appears to have remained relatively the same as it was under the guidance of Don Bartolo. "Even though I was deprived of all assistance, I can say that, by the grace of God, I was at Naples what I had been in Venice," Eugène wrote of his spiritual state during his year in Naples. If his spiritual life had taken any sort of negative turn in Naples, Eugène's passionate personality would have almost certainly mentioned it later in his retreat notes from his time in seminary or early in his priesthood. Resources were lacking to carry out the other directives of Don Bartolo. There was not enough money for Eugène's education to continue, and the only means of satisfying Don Bartolo's other recommendation, quality friendships, was his nightly visits to the home of family friends. There he encountered individuals who helped expand his intellect slightly, but did little to help him grow in his spiritual life.

On one of these occasions, Eugène spoke with a Marquis who appeared to enjoy his chat with Eugène. When he complimented Charles-Antoine de Mazenod on the intellect of his son, Eugène's father responded by telling the Marquis that he was only sixteen. Eugène chided his father for telling the Marquis this, fearing that, in the future, everyone would look upon him as a child whose thoughts and opinions were not to be taken seriously. He felt out of place in these gatherings and like no one understood him. The comments from his father did not help Eugène with his inner struggle. This pain, coupled with the troubles within his family, damaged the still-evolving psychological makeup of young Eugène de Mazenod. Most troublesome of all, there was no one around to help Eugène through the struggles he was enduring.

The young Frenchman did make the acquaintance of a young man who took him on a few trips here and there, but aside from that, he had no virtuous companions and no aids to grow in holiness or to engage in academic studies. Sixteen-year-old Eugène de Mazenod was trapped in an inescapable state of idleness. "What a wretched existence for a sixteen-year-old: nothing to do, not knowing what to do with oneself, no friends, not able to see anything," he wrote years later.

Alteration of the Call

Don Bartolo Zinelli entered religious life in 1798, the same year Eugène lived in Naples. The young priest joined the Society of the Priests of the Faith, a group of religious attempting to re-establish the Jesuit order.[25] The letters Zinelli sent to his former pupil encouraged Eugène to join Don Bartolo in pursuing religious life. What little remains in existence of Eugène's responses to these overtures seems to assert that Eugène did not want to join the Society of the Priests of the Faith. His desire to be a priest, if it still existed in Naples, no longer included entering the missionary field, even though Eugène later wrote that he would have followed Don Bartolo into religious life had he stayed in Venice a year longer.

Dramatic Escape from Naples

The de Mazenods left Naples in a hurry. In late December of 1798, they received word from the Queen that she and her Court were fleeing the city due to the inevitable invasion of the French army. The de Mazenods were offered a place on one of the Queen's ships, but Charles-Antoine instead accepted a similar offer from a Portuguese admiral.

The task of accompanying the family's luggage to the ship fell to Eugène. As in Venice, the attitude of the locals towards French refugees had turned against them. While on the way to the port, he was able to avoid being tied up and held captive by the locals only because he was accompanied by Portuguese sailors. Other Frenchmen trying to flee were not as fortunate. When he reached the port, Eugène met resistance from those guarding the entrance to the port and was forced to get tough and use some trickery to get his family's belongings on the Portuguese flagship.

---

[25] The Society of the Priests of the Faith did not succeed in re-establishing the Jesuit order. While the Jesuit order did return, it was not revived by the group Don Bartolo joined. The founder of the Society of the Priests of the Faith started off admirably in his work, but then fell into disrepute. The failure of the Society of the Priests of the Faith is the reason Saint Eugène de Mazenod gave as to why Don Bartolo was never and will never be canonized.

While Eugène was completing this errand, a friend of Charles-Antoine had visited the house and told them about a young Frenchman who had been killed while trying to take a cart of his belongings to the port. His family feared it was Eugène who had been lynched, but just as their friend had finished the story, Eugène arrived to report that he had completed his task.

In the middle of the night, the Portuguese snuck his family out of their house and took them aboard the ship. However, stormy weather prevented them from leaving for eight days. During this time, the family stayed on the boat, but Eugène went back onto shore to settle some final business matters and sell items the family would be unable to take with them.

When the time finally came to depart, Eugène had to rush back to the ship in the middle of the night and take a barge over the stormy water to re-board the anchored ship off in the harbor. As waves crashed over the sides of the barge, his family and the sailors on the ship watched in horror, thinking the barge would capsize and Eugène would drown, but Eugène remained calm and used a bucket to bail out the boat. Once Eugène was on the ship again, they waited until morning to depart. Then they set sail from Naples on January 3, 1799, and arrived in Palermo on January 6.

The Cannizzaro Family

Modest Lodgings

Upon arriving in Palermo, the de Mazenods learned that Ferdinand IV had ordered all French émigrés to leave Palermo. They were to be deported during the night of January 7 or early in the morning of January 8. For a third time, the de Mazenod family had been under threat of deportation when they arrived in a new city, and for a third time, Charles-Antoine de Mazenod's connections helped them avoid such an ordeal. The kindness of Queen Marie-Caroline of Naples came through again, as she had made arrangements to exempt the de Mazenod family from the deportation order.

When the de Mazenods disembarked from the boat, they were unable to find lodgings because all of the hotels in the city were full. They accepted an offer to share a room in the house of a friend until a permanent dwelling could be acquired. Once again, financial restraints created an impediment to finding adequate housing. In a sly manner and sensitive to the pride of the de Mazenods, the Queen of Naples assisted them once more by sending Fortuné 25 onces (equivalent to 325 francs) asking him to say Mass for her.

The Cannizzaro Family

In Palermo, the de Mazenods entered high society and socialized with many of the most prominent families in the area. Among the more notable acquaintances of the de Mazenods were Baldassare Platamone and Moncada Branciforte (the princess of Larderia), Duke and Duchess of Cannizzaro. The Cannizzaro family had two sons who were slightly younger than Eugène. They became friends, and Eugène took on a role as a mentor and surrogate brother to the boys. The duchess was pleased with the positive influence the young Frenchman had on her sons.[26] Soon, Eugène was adopted into the Cannizzaro family, and he began to spend most of his time living with them.

Living with his adopted family was a welcome change for Eugène. The poverty he experienced in Venice and Naples took its toll on the young Frenchman, and he reveled in the lavish living conditions of the duke and duchess' home:

> I am, my dear Papa, living like a prize gamecock; an excellent bed, a charming room, a dressing room, etc., a valet at my disposal who, only this morning, pressed my clothes. (A very important matter.)…This morning when I awoke, it was like being out in the beautiful open fields, so delightful is the view from my room. Family and servants alike do everything in their power to anticipate my every wish.

The luxury he experienced was not the main reason Eugène enjoyed the Cannizzaro home. His favorite part was the mother-son bond he formed with Duchess Cannizzaro. "[H]er own children could not have loved her more than I did," he later wrote. She became his second mother. He was separated from his mother and had been without a mother figure for years. Living in a completely different country from his mother took its toll on Eugène. Despite the great love Eugène had for his father and uncles, he was missing the influence of a mother in his life. He was in need of a mother figure, and Duchess

---

[26] Based on Eugène's account, it appears these two boys needed moral guidance and slid into immorality when Eugène returned to France.

Cannizzaro desired someone who could mentor her sons, to help them grow in virtue. These complimentary desires and Divine Providence brought Saint Eugène de Mazenod and Duchess Cannizzaro together, and a familial bond formed.

Attempts to Remedy Educational Neglect

While living with the Cannizzaros and being integrated into the Palermitan high society, Eugène more fully realized his lack of an education and began to remedy the situation. He often read to and with the duchess which gave him exposure to literature. The Cannizzaros also gave him unlimited access to their library. However, Eugène had no guidance with respect to his choices in books. His father did not always approve of the literature he was reading, and sometimes Charles-Antoine had to explain to Eugène the errors contained in the works he was reading. Eugène had no spiritual guidance with regards to his choice in reading materials either. The Cannizzaros did have a family chaplain, but Eugène did not care for him. "A stupid individual! He scarcely knows how to read," he wrote of him to his father. As a result of this lack of spiritual guidance, Eugène's knowledge of theology and spiritual matters suffered instead of flourishing. Furthermore, Eugène took up the study of history in addition to his exploration of literature.

However, not all of Eugène's new educational opportunities came from reading and studying. He took advantage of the hunting and horse-riding lessons offered by his adoptive brothers' tutor. Also, simply living in a foreign land provided him with an educational opportunity.

The years of living in cities that are now a part of a unified Italy brought Eugène into daily contact with the Italian language. Despite his early struggles with the language in Nice, he had mastered the language by the time he was in Palermo. His father wrote to his sister that Eugène spoke and wrote in Italian "better than most of the Italians themselves." In 1801, he even earned a commission to revise the text of a work an Italian scholar had translated from French into Italian.

Eugène's Behavior in Palermo

Through his association with the Cannizzaro family, Eugène crossed paths with many in the royal and noble class, which exposed Eugène to the grandeur and morally precarious lifestyle of the upper class in Palermo. Eugène felt drawn to the class superiority expressed by those he encountered at the social gatherings. He felt the need to have a noble title like everyone else and chose to stylize himself as the Count de Mazenod, despite no such title existing in his family. In Naples, Eugène felt everyone viewed him as an immature child, and he overcompensated in Palermo by trying to establish himself as a mature, young nobleman and embracing the high society in which he found himself. This environment inflated Eugène's ego, something that would need to be tamed in the future for the purposes of sanctification.

During this period of his life, Eugène was criticized by his family for his behavior. Letters written by Charles-Antoine to him reveal Eugène's struggle with arrogance, compassion, and temper. Furthermore, Eugène's father warned the young count to avoid over indulgence.

The lifestyle of Palermo was a major source of concern for not only Charles-Antoine, but also Ninette, Eugène's sister. Her letters to Eugène expressed concern over the abundance of amusements that occurred in Palermo. Ninette's concerns were unnecessary, however.

While he struggled with haughtiness and elitism, Saint Eugène, in his memoirs, wrote of his distaste for the immoral habits of the aristocracy in Palermo. In fact, when he found himself at a social gathering that was rife with frivolity and dissipation, a great sadness would come over him, and he would withdraw from the crowd. If an acquaintance found him in this condition, nothing could succeed in drawing him out of his melancholic state. Eugène reported:

I was out of my element. I felt as though I were being forcefully thrust into a world towards which I felt no attraction. I hated the dissipation I saw all around me, for it was repugnant to all the yearnings of my soul for an entirely different kind of happiness. The greater the dissipation I saw in others, all the more strongly did I yearn for the opposite. That is the only way I can explain this phenomenon.

High society in Palermo appealed to Eugène's instincts as a nobleman, but the grace of God had instilled in Eugène's heart a longing that the social scene could not fulfill. The lifestyle of the Palermitan aristocracy was abhorrent to him. He was out of place. From his assignment in the Society of the Priests of the Faith, Don Bartolo wrote him, advising to do "[n]othing against God; nothing without God." Eugène tried his best to follow his tutor's advice. His confessor was a bishop, and he avoided socializing with females as much as possible to avoid falling into sins of lust, always distancing himself from the young ladies he encountered at social engagements and fighting off whatever advances they made. Eugène believed that friendships with women "find their origin more in the senses than in the heart."

Eugène's chaste behavior was both the subject of jokes and praise from those he encountered in Palermo's elite social class. On one occasion, Eugène was asked to escort a young lady home from a party because she lived near the de Mazenod residence. To the great amusement of those in attendance, Eugène became embarrassed and declined to do so. Nevertheless, they insisted, and he awkwardly took her arm and escorted her home. Eugène had no knowledge of the proper etiquette for walking a young lady home. He knew he did not want those passing by to think he was engaging in scandalous activities, so whenever they encountered a carriage, he made the young girl hide from the lights of the carriage. The young girl was so struck by this odd behavior that she could not help but tell others about it. Eugène's father upon hearing the story chided him for using excessive modesty, but everyone in Palermo could agree his intentions were in the right place. As time passed, Eugène became less awkward around women as he gained more experience spending time in the company of females, especially the Duchess Cannizzaro who had a significant impact on his behavior.

During his time in Palermo, Eugène found in the Cannizzaro home an environment fit for practicing virtue. Watching over the piety of the Cannizzaro boys helped Eugène keep his own piety intact. Furthermore, the duchess gave Eugène the responsibility of carrying out her charitable activities. She spent a good portion of her income on alleviating the woes of the poor in Palermo. By executing these works of charity, Eugène became more aware of the waste that was occurring in Palermo's high society. Helping Duchess Cannizzaro give to the poor was not the only charitable practice he undertook, however. Eugène, on more than one occasion, was at the bedside of sick friends, caring for them. He even held a young girl as she died of tuberculosis, showing no concern for his own health. A letter from Charles-Antoine to Marie-Rose reports the concern and care Eugène gave to an ailing family friend:

> I assure you that I was indeed proud of my son, under the circumstances. He forsook all the enjoyments of the Carnival, as well as others, to come and stay at the home of our good friends and to care for the dear patient with skill, devotion, and affection. And this wasn't the only time he did such a thing. He has done just as much for other friends on several occasions, which only goes to prove how kind he is.

Care for the sick appears to be a pattern of behavior for Eugène while living with Duchess Cannizzaro. He sacrificed socializing and risked his own health to care for others. Contagious diseases did not frighten the young man who would later found a missionary society dedicated to serving the most abandoned souls.

The Death of the Duchess

One other individual Eugène aided while she was on her deathbed was none other than the Duchess Cannizzaro. In May of 1802, he sat up with her one Friday night until two in the morning. He went to visit her again the next day at eleven, but she was still asleep. Eugène decided to return later and went for a haircut. When he returned, Eugène discovered she had passed away just moments before his arrival and he fell down at the foot of her bed crying, "I have lost my mother! I have lost my mother!"

Under these tragic circumstances, Eugène's conduct was praised by his family, but interiorly Eugène was crushed. "The blow was cruel and the wound deep," Eugène wrote. "I felt it for a long time; it even made me ill." In the letters he composed at the time, Eugène wrote of the great number of tears he shed over losing his second mother. For consolation, he began reading *The Nights* by Edward Young. His father discouraged him from reading that text and reminded him of the truths of his faith, hoping he would find comfort in knowing that the duchess' saintly life must have surely been rewarded with the Beatific Vision. This reminder from his father was unable to take root in his heart, and his grief only worsened.

Eugène's conduct may have been praised by others at this time, but he began to grow lukewarm in his faith. He still fulfilled his obligations, but his interior faith sputtered. His writings from that time period show no inklings of religious sentiment. The duchess was his model of virtue. Without her example, Eugène fell into a state of gloom that would eventually spiral downwards into a profound spiritual crisis.

Return to France

Called Home

During the final days of the life of Duchess Cannizzaro and while Eugène mourned her loss, another conflict was reaching its climax. His parents were fighting over him and where he ought to live. Marie-Rose desired to see her son return to France and live with her, while Charles-Antoine resisted her demands.

Previously, Marie-Rose had expressed a desire to be reunited with not only Eugène, but also her husband and brothers-in-law. By 1800, however, her only concern was getting Eugène away from the de Mazenod men whom the Joannis family considered undesirable with respect to raising Eugène. The Joannis family's irritation with Charles-Antoine increased over his refusal to send Eugène back to France. For a brief time in 1801, however, news of how well the Cannizzaros were taking care of Eugène as well as financial strains diminished Marie-Rose's eagerness to see Eugène returned to her. Her wavering on the issue continued for some time, but her desire to have Eugène return to France eventually became non-negotiable.

Charles-Antoine, on the other hand, was more even-tempered, despite suffering from the discussion of sending Eugène away to his mother. He always remained open to the idea, but insisted that Marie-Rose reveal her motivations for calling Eugène back to France. For a considerable time, she refused to explain her reasoning to Charles-Antoine, perhaps to avoid telling him of her family's hatred for him and his brothers.

In May of 1802, the same month Duchess Cannizzaro passed away, Marie-Rose finally gave Charles-Antoine an explanation for why she needed Eugène to leave exile. The Joannis family had arranged for a marriage with a young girl who was described as having a "fine figure" and a pleasant personality. The chief reason the Joannis family wanted Eugène to marry her, however, was her dowry. The young lady brought with her an annual income of 25,000 livres. Once Eugène was married, Marie-Rose explained to Charles-Antoine, the Joannis family would find a husband for Ninette. Only after their children's financial positions were secured would Marie-Rose consider allowing Charles-Antoine and his brothers to return to France. The next month, Charles-Antoine sent a letter to Marie-Rose, agreeing to send Eugène back to France as soon as the Joannis family sent the money to pay for his trip.

Eugène's return to his native country was the final step in the complete break between Charles-Antoine de Mazenod and Marie-Rose. The hope of reuniting with his wife to which Charles-Antoine had previously clung was now gone. Marie-Rose had taken everything from him: his daughter, his money, and now his son.

Eugène's Departure

It would be a few months before arrangements could be made for Eugène's return journey to France. In order to obtain a passport to return to France, Eugène was required to take an oath of loyalty to France and the country's new leader, Napoleon Bonaparte. Signing this oath meant agreeing to refrain from sending mail to enemies of France, which included all of the noblemen who had fled during the French Revolution. Eugène detested Napoleon's government and had no desire whatsoever to pledge allegiance to a man he called a "despot," nor did he like the idea of vowing to not write his father and uncles. Yet, the desire to see his mother again proved strong enough to allow him to reluctantly sign the oath. A severe illness further delayed his return, but he was finally ready to return to France by October of 1802.

On the day of Eugène's departure, his heartbroken father and uncles escorted him to his ship. Marie-Rose had requested that Fortuné accompany Eugène back to France, but he chose to stay behind with his brothers. The three de Mazenod brothers watched the ship carry Eugène away from Palermo and away from them, then slowly walked back to their lodgings which must have seemed empty without the youthful energy of Eugène.

A Difficult Journey

On board the ship that was to carry him back to France, Eugène's excitement to see his mother, sister, and grandmother again faded and was replaced by grief over leaving his father and uncles. As the ship pulled away from the shore, tears filled his eyes. Throughout Eugène's journey, he could not cease crying. His weeping caused him to lose sleep. Eugène even found it difficult to write a letter to his father and uncles, for his tears were dripping onto the paper.

The travel conditions were far from comfortable during the two weeks he spent at sea, making his dreary journey even worse. The boat was cold, and the food served on board was tasteless. His friends in Palermo had offered him food for the journey, but out of pride, he had refused everything except for some chocolate and some preserves, hardly enough to satisfy his hunger. He soon found himself regretting his refusal of the snacks. Furthermore, a storm put the ship in grave danger one night.

Confusion in Marseilles

Eleven years of exile and two miserable weeks on a ship were at an end. As his ship pulled into the port of Marseilles, Eugène, now twenty years old, felt excited to begin life anew in his native country. His immediate concern, though, was reuniting with his mother. It had been seven years since he had last seen her, and she had been the driving force behind leaving his father behind and returning to the country of his birth.

When his ship arrived at the port city where he would one day serve as bishop, he stepped off and scanned the crowd searching for his mother. She was nowhere to be found. The happy reunion he had expected did not occur. Instead, Eugène de Mazenod was greeted by a feeling of bitter disappointment.

Eugène then made his way to an associate of his father who informed him that arrangements had been made for him at the home of a Madame Estieu. There he found a note from his mother explaining that there were some things she needed him to do for her in Marseilles.

Over the course of the next four days, Eugène completed all that his mother had instructed him to do in Marseilles and took care of some tasks his father requested of him, as well. Not once during those four days in Marseilles did he see or hear from anyone in the Joannis family. Perturbed by the lack of communication from his mother and unable to wait any longer, he made the decision to return to Aix on his own.

Upon hearing of the neglect of his son in Marseilles, Charles-Antoine de Mazenod became outraged and demanded an explanation from his wife. Marie-Rose provided no response. Instead, Eugène was forced to provide the reason, plunging Eugène into a situation to which many children in modern society can relate—passing messages between their divorced parents. Eugène told his father the lack of instructions resulted from an error within the postal service. The unreliability of the postal service of the day makes this excuse plausible, but the temperament of the Joannis family raises doubts to its truth.

Disappointment in Aix

Under the new French law, émigrés were subject to residence surveillance, so when he arrived in Aix-en-Provence, Eugène was whisked away to his grandmother's home in Saint-Julien to wait for Roze Joannis to escort him to the de Mazenod's country estate in Saint-Laurent. Once he was registered as a citizen there, Eugène could find a substitute for the now mandatory military service that would be required of him at a much lower cost than if he had been living in Aix. The reunion with his mother was brief and not nearly as happy as he imagined it would be.

Eugène's disappointment would continue for several weeks. He spent two weeks waiting at his grandmother's home before Roze was available to take him to Saint-Laurent. It must have been an annoyance for Eugène to wait for Roze before traveling, as he had just made a journey from Marseilles to Aix on his own. But, obedient to his mother and excited to be reunited with his grandmother whom he loved dearly, he endured the two weeks of waiting. When Roze brought him to Saint-Laurent, he established himself as a resident as quickly as possible. By the time he was able to return to Aix, it was nearly Christmas. However, he soon needed to return to Saint-Laurent after spending only six months with his mother and sister. Young men were being conscripted into military service, and Eugène once again needed to prove he was a resident of Saint-Laurent. He left Aix in a hurry to prove his residence once more and allow for a replacement to be found.

Eugène found himself stuck in Saint-Laurent for approximately six months because the conscription kept getting postponed. There were no books to read and nothing to do other than to observe the conditions of his father's land. He attempted to improve the property and control the less than admirable farmers his mother had settled on the land, but he was out of his element and unable to make the improvements he desired. "I cannot stand it anymore, dearest papa; I am dying of boredom," Eugène complained to his father in a letter dated September 21, 1803. "It is three long months since I have been in splendid isolation in this place, bored with the country and its inhabitants." Eugène was alone, and the Joannis family did nothing to ease his troublesome existence in the country.

No one from his family visited Eugène during his time in Saint-Laurent. Marie-Rose vacationed with Roze, but did not visit her son. Eugène's loneliness and irritation prompted him to write his mother, "Before returning to France, had I foreseen that I should have to dwell on the mountain apart, I would never have left where I was, for what prompted me to make the move was my desire to be near you and to live with you." This desire had not been realized, but after everything had been arranged and the government was satisfied, Eugène was finally reunited with his mother and sister in Aix and was able to forget the whole ordeal.

Spiritual Crisis

A Failed Attempt to Reunite His Parents

In Aix, Eugène immediately began attempting to reunite his parents. His first step was to recover the inheritance from his granduncle Charles-André's estate and settle the debts incurred by the de Mazenod family. The money gained from the inheritance was enough to pay for his father and uncles' travel expenses. The laws Napoleon had set in place had made it easier for him to recover the money confiscated by the government and for émigrés to return to France without legal penalties. It was time consuming work for Eugène (although, he did manage to find the time to squeeze in a little study of history and the French, Italian, and Latin languages), but he eventually managed to arrive at a position where there was no financial or legal obstacle to the return of Charles-Antoine de Mazenod and his brothers. The only task that remained for Eugène was to mend the ill-will his parents had for one another.

Despite all Eugène could do to clear the way for his father's return, Charles-Antoine refused to end his exile. The terms Marie-Rose laid down for Charles-Antoine's return were unacceptable to him. She did not want Charles-Antoine or his brothers near her. If they returned, she demanded they live in the house in Saint-Laurent while she lived in Aix. Charles-Antoine would not allow a scandal like that. Neither would compromise on their demands, and Eugène resigned himself to the fact many children in today's world have to face—that his parents would never get back together.

Life With the Joannis Family

Living with the Joannis family was a big adjustment for Eugène. It is fair to say he never completely adjusted to their way of life. He was used to the way things were while he was living with the de Mazenod men, and because he had a personality similar to his father's, he preferred it to the lifestyle of his maternal family. The Joannis clan, recognizing how similar his personality was to his father's, intended to mold him into a true Joannis rather than accept him for who he was.

All this caused Eugène to realize he was, at times, a pawn in the struggle between the paternal and maternal sides of his family. Both the de Mazenod and Joannis families loved him, but the bitterness between them created tension. Eugène felt tempted to compare the two families and choose which one he liked more. While he did not love his paternal family more than his maternal family, he, nevertheless, preferred the way he was treated and shown affection by the de Mazenods over the approach taken by the Joannis family, and the lack of understanding he received from the Joannis side of his family frustrated him.

In the Joannis house, much like it was in Nice, Marie-Rose, along with her mother and sister, made all decisions. Any opposition was met with a fierce uprising from the three women. Life with his mother, aunt, and grandmother was further agitated by their propensities to throw fits whenever things did not go their way. His mother was especially moody, and her ever-changing health exacerbated her irritability.[27] Marie-Rose's sister, Gabrielle Élisabeth Dedons de Pierrefeu, was even more

---

[27] Marie-Rose often fell ill and suffered from what was described as nervous disorders. A modern-day mental health professional would have given her a different psychological diagnosis. Without

prone to temper tantrums, and often locked herself in her room, threatening to kill herself. On one such occasion, Eugène had to break down her door and force her to drink a glass of water.

The one respite Eugène had from the dismal state of life with the Joannis women was his sister Ninette. She was the one on whom Eugène could count for support and a good laugh. When Eugène was trying to force his aunt to drink the water, she was standing to the side, making faces at him.

It cannot be said, though, that the Joannis women intended to alienate Eugène. They were kind and loving to him most of the time. Eugène wrote fondly of his mother and grandmother to his father and truly loved them. His struggles with them are not indicative of how he felt about them or how they felt about him. Marie-Rose and her mother[28] both loved Eugène. Yet, it was their mutual love for each other that caused their disagreements to be all the more painful.

For the most part, Eugène tried to hide from his father the pains he felt from life with the maternal side of his family. There were moments, though, where he did tell his father of his

---

being able to observe the behavior first-hand, it is nearly impossible to provide an accurate description of her symptoms.

[28] Élisabeth Joannis spoiled Eugène. He judged her not by her faults, but by the great love she had for him. Describing the pain he felt upon her death on August 15, 1811, he said, "Never was a mother more tenderly loved than I loved her. Hence, her death was for me the most harrowing trial that I have ever endured. I never knew anyone more perfect on earth." As evidenced by her treatment of Charles-Antoine and his brothers, she was far from perfect. If her death elicited that moving of a response from Eugène, she must have had some admirable qualities, for Eugène did not eulogize his aunt in a similar manner. He expressed doubts as to the fate of Élisabeth Dedons de Pierrefeu's soul when she died on June 7, 1807.

anguish. Once, the actions of his mother caused him to snap and vent:

> Can it be that no one understands me? Is it conceivable that my own mother does not appreciate me? That may sound insolent to you, but they force me to say it. To be perfectly truthful, my mother tries my patience before she has anything to complain about. She should have—and they'll end up by making me bad enough to wish to inflict it on her—I repeat, she should have a son like many others I know; then she would really have nothing to complain about. Must I sing my own praises around here, or write out my own defense? It's a sorry state of affairs when my own family does not share the opinion everyone else has of me, and it's a justly deserved one, I might say. Why not be honest about it? If fulfilling every duty, forsaking every distraction, and practicing self-restraint on every occasion, if all these are enough to entitle anyone to a good opinion, why do they want more? My mother can thank God that my principles are too solidly grounded ever to permit me to put them aside. For, she can be perfectly sure that were my behavior something put on, I would long ago have indulged in any pleasure I might have gained from showing her the difference between a son like myself, and one such as they could very well force me to be…but, she need not have worries on that score. I do not doubt that my mother loves me very much, but, by doing so, she is merely fulfilling an obligation imposed upon her by nature; I might say by gratitude also, since no son could love his mother as I love mine. Perhaps the family here doubts this because I love others besides my mother. Let me make myself clear. There is no obligation which says I should love no one but my mother; but, because I do love others, this family imagines, in fact it is convinced, that I love her less than I should, and one member of the family dared to berate me for it. In all

fairness to my mother, she has never given me any cause to suspect that she feels this way; and yet, there is a small consolation in that, since, far from sparing my feelings, they have let me know from time to time that I have no voice in the family, and will have none until after my mother, who now gives all the orders, dies. And it hurts me very much to hear my mother say, "You can do as you please when I am gone."…She wants me to feel completely dependent upon her, and, therefore, that I should behave accordingly. You know me fairly well. Do you think this precaution is necessary? Do you think it is even wise for anyone to resort to means of this kind? Frankly, if I were more heartless and had no regard for what pleases or grieves this family, don't they realize that I could soon become independent of them? Again I say, how little they know me. They trust in weapons of which I have little fear, while, all the time, their guarantee of victory lies in my heart.

Here the temper of Saint Eugène shows through. His frustrations boil over, yet at the end of the letter we see him soften. The tail end shows us just how much love he had in his heart; he recognized the fact that his tender heart would prevent him from rebelling against the mother he loved so much.

In response to this letter, Charles-Antoine reminded Eugène that both of his parents loved him, but, because of the differences in their personalities, they expressed it in different ways. Charles-Antoine went on to say that he believed Marie-Rose was, by nature, a kind person, but that she was easily influenced. Furthermore, he assured Eugène that he had been behaving as he should and that he should continue to do so.

Stifled and Bored

Eugène grew frustrated in the Joannis home. His mother, grandmother, and aunt concentrated on business, financial affairs, household issues, and other matters that bored Eugène.

Life with his father and encountering other nobles in Italy had widened his interests. He longed for an escape from the monotony, something to entertain him.

Initially, Eugène embraced everything the social scene in Aix had to offer. He went with friends to musical comedies and to dances. It was not long before Eugène saw the vanity of these activities and became bored with them. The musical comedies only entertained him because the performers constantly tried to upstage one another. The shows, dances, and social scene left him feeling empty and alone. Soon, Eugène began spending almost all his time at home, longing for something more. He found a tiny bit of solace by imagining himself talking with his father and uncles during the solitary walks he took through the city of Aix.

Eugène spent his days at home because he did not fit in the new France Napoleon Bonaparte was creating. In Eugène's mind, he deserved to be in a highly respectable position, but to do so meant serving an emperor whom he despised. His efforts to take his mind off this problematic situation failed. Eugène wrote to his father in February of 1804 of his frustrations:

> It is true that I am taking advantage of the entertainments this city offers me. By this means I keep myself in a daze with regard to the prospect of being condemned to inaction, but for all that I still harbor the desire to take up a career of some kind. In the meantime, the days and the years flow by.

Eugène longed for something more, but was unable to find it. No career available to him satisfied his desires. He found himself in the same type of quarter-life crisis that many millennials are enduring today. Eugène felt unsure of what he should do with his life, but he knew the career paths available to him would not satisfy his desires.

Lack of Virtuous Friendships

During his quarter-life crisis, Eugène longed for a group of friends (or even just one) with whom he could share his struggles. He could not relate to the Joannis women, and letters to his father took months to arrive if they arrived at all. Only friendship could give him solace in the midst of his internal anguish, but Eugène's high standards for his friends made finding one difficult. Describing his ideal friend, Eugène wrote:

> I have always longed for a friend, but I have never found one, at least one such as I am seeking; it is true that I am hard to please for as it is my nature to give generously I expect the same in return. Even so I do not spurn some friendships of an ordinary, less exalted kind, although they are not really to my taste. In such cases, I give in proportion to what I think I might experience in return…All those stories from history that tell of various similar examples of heroic friendships make my heart sing for joy; at that moment, I experience a longing in my heart to meet such a treasure. In short, I need to love and as I know inside me what a truly perfect love would be like, I will not ever be satisfied with those ordinary friendships which are good enough for most people. I aim at a friendship which, to sum it all up in a word, would make but one being where there were two.

Eugène found a taste of the benefits of a virtuous friendship in his Venetian spiritual mentor and teacher Don Bartolo Zinelli. His lonely year in Naples that separated him from Don Bartolo created an intense longing for friendship. Other than the Duchess Cannizzaro, he experienced nothing in Naples or Palermo that resembled what he desired in a friendship. When he returned to Aix, Eugène found himself in the same situation, longing for quality friendships, but he found no friendship that would satisfy him, no one to whom he could turn with his interior struggles, and no friend that would help him grow in holiness. The plans Eugène's family formulated for him to marry also failed to provide an adequate companion.

Marriage Plans Fall Apart

Eugène believed that marriage would allow him to escape the stifling atmosphere of life with the Joannis women. This reduced his feelings towards a potential marriage to that of a business transaction. The failure of his parents' marriage, which had been arranged in a similar manner (i.e., for financial and social gain), did not, as one might assume, deter him from marrying solely for selfish reasons. In Eugène's mind, the most important quality for a potential spouse was the size of her dowry.

There were two scenarios placed before him to achieve his goals. Before he had returned to France, his mother and the Joannis family had found for him a potential wife who was described by Marie-Rose as "richer beyond all expectations." Eugène, noticing her appealing physical appearance and liking the size of her dowry, consented to the marriage. However, just as the plans were about to be finalized, the young girl suddenly passed away. Eugène scoffed at the idea of marrying the second girl his family found for him, for she was not nearly as wealthy as he would have liked. "40,000 francs, when I want 150,000!" he wrote to his father. "And middle class! How do you think that fits in with my plans? If they cannot do better than that, I'm afraid I shall die a virgin, if you'll pardon the expression."

After the second attempt to marry failed, Eugène lost what little interest he had in marriage. "It is not that I do not want to have a lot of little children, but the wife!" he wrote to his father. "Ah! A wife is a terrible thing! And then again, there is the fact that I want her to be very rich, very rich and good. That combination is very hard to find. You can see, then, my dear papa, that your wishes run the risk of remaining in the oven for a long time yet."

Eugène expressed a distaste in marriage found in many children of divorced parents. With no example in one's home of how beautiful the Sacrament of Matrimony can be, it is difficult to find a desire to enter into a marital bond knowing how much pain a failed marriage can cause. While this, no doubt, played a role in his distaste for marriage, the failure of his parents' marriage might not have been the main source of these feelings. God created Saint Eugène de Mazenod to be a priest. Therefore, marriage would not satisfy the desires of his heart.

Self-inflicted Exile?

Having found no suitable wife in France to escape living with the Joannis family, Eugène became desperate to find a better life and restore himself to the aristocratic lifestyle to which he felt entitled. He began planning to return to Sicily and use his father's connections to obtain a favorable post in the Palatine military. When he learned of his son's plans, Charles-Antoine de Mazenod warned Eugène of potential difficulties in obtaining a respectable position and the near insurmountable opposition that would come from his mother and grandmother.

In spite of the difficulties, Eugène was determined to leave France. With an air of elitism that had been awakened in his soul, he explained to his father, "I always visualized glory as my goal, the respect of good people as a reward; if I have attained the first one, it is proof that I am worthy of the second." In his own mind, Eugène was destined for greatness. He could not achieve that end in Napoleon's France, making the move back to Italy a necessary course of action.

Following the advice of his father, Eugène planned to go to Palermo, telling his mother that he was just going to visit his father and uncles. Once in Palermo, he would write to his mother in an attempt to persuade her to allow him to stay and to send money to help him establish a satisfactory lifestyle.

Eugène's plan appears to have been destined for failure before he could even begin to execute it. At that time, it was difficult for young men, especially the sons of émigrés, to obtain a passport. While on vacation in Paris, Eugène met with a French official named Portalis, the Minister of Public Worship, who offered him a post in the government and made promises to help out his father and uncles, when they were able to return to France. Eugène abhorred the idea of working for Napoleon, but acted as if he was interested in order to obtain a passport under the guise of wishing to consult his father on the offer. The minister was more than willing to obtain that for him, but in order to do so, he needed the Minister of Police, Fouché, to sign off on the passport. However, Portalis and Fouché were in the midst of a bitter feud. Eugène, just as he had with his parents, became a tool that two feuding individuals could use against one another. The passport was denied, and Eugène's plans fell apart.

Perpetuated Painful Separation From His Father

During Eugène's time in Paris, he spoke to some acquaintances who eased his concerns about the new government. He began to warm up to the idea of staying in France, accepting the position offered to him, and arranging to have his father return to France. With no way to obtain a passport, it was impossible for Eugène to speak with his father and uncles in person to properly explain to them why they should return to France. Charles-Antoine refused to return to France, telling Eugène that Marie-Rose "simply did not want her brothers-in-law or her husband near her." The defeat of his plans was demoralizing in and of itself, but Eugène's pain was compounded by the realization he might not ever get to see his father again.

Eugène suffered greatly from the absence of his father. When a later possibility for a reunion with his father failed, he wrote:

> With delight I see arriving the happy moment when I can embrace you once again after twelve years of a painful separation. I am counting the minutes; my joy is at fever pitch;

I cannot conceive that anything could now obstruct our happiness. My soul is given over entirely and exclusively to this hope. And then, suddenly, as if with a violent motion, an opposing will jerks away these sweet dreams. My heart is bruised. It feels the pain all that much more deeply because it cannot hide the fact that the reasons given for this opposition are decisive. It understands the detrimental impact a postponement of its happiness can have on the interests of the people who are dear to him.

Eugène could find no way to reunite himself with his father and began to come to terms with the reality that he might not ever get to see him again. His acceptance of the facts did not lessen the pain he felt.

Problems Create More Problems

Eugène de Mazenod had been forced out of his native country, driving his family into exile and poverty. The somewhat nomadic lifestyle his family was forced to live while in exile separated him from his spiritual and educational mentor. His parents divorced, and he found himself separated from his mother. The woman who had become his second mother died. His mother demanded that he return to France, separating him from his father. He could not find a career that satisfied him or an adequate wife. Eugène's attempts to bring his father back to France and reunite his parents were unsuccessful. All his plans for his life and for his family failed to come to fruition. The many disappointments and struggles of his life combined to make life miserable, and storm clouds began to form in the soul of Saint Eugène de Mazenod.

It is clear that Eugène was in a dangerous place psychologically speaking. In March of 1804, Eugène reported to his father that he was feeling "misanthropic" and that "nothing gives me any pleasure. I have a heavy case of aversion to this part of the world." A month later he wrote, "I get angry when I see the best years of my life draining away in idle obscurity." The separation from his father only compounded his anxieties:

> I cannot hide the fact that I do not have the courage to face the challenge of this new trial and that the courage and resignation with which up to now I have withstood blows of every description are failing me on this occasion. Separated from people who form part of me, the happiness of keeping in touch by means of correspondence that is very dear to me has helped me wait in patience for the happy moment of our reunion for which I am continually longing…can we really bring ourselves to make the coldblooded decision that we will not see each other ever again before the day of the Resurrection?

When a young man enters a crisis like the one Eugène was enduring, he needs his father or another paternal figure in his life to help guide him through the turbulence. However, the only father figure Eugène had was the Jansenist Roze Joannis, who did care for Eugène but was a woefully inadequate substitute for his father.

Spiritual Crisis

The struggles and challenges Eugène endured upon his return to France further agitated a problem that had been brewing since the death of the Duchess Cannizzaro. The pains of Eugène's personal life caused a deeper need for a strong spiritual life, but at that time, his spiritual life was sputtering. Saint Eugène de Mazenod provides little detail of this spiritual crisis in his memoirs and the notes he took while on retreats, but he, without a doubt, endured one.

This struggle affected only Eugène's spiritual approach to the Faith. He remained fervent in his theological beliefs and often debated the Jansenist Roze Joannis, as well as peers who supported the ideas of Voltaire. He even took up a private study of these issues so as to better prepare himself for the debates with Roze. Also unharmed was his moral character. His mother, who was often critical of his personality and attitudes, attested that he was a well-behaved young man.

The struggle was interior and almost unnoticeable to others. Therefore, his parents were unable to fully comprehend the entirety of what Eugène felt and experienced. His faith, which had been so fervent in Venice, was now merely an obligation to fulfill. Eugène was no longer motivated by a desire for God and the betterment of those around him. He still prayed, but it did not move him to live his faith out as it did in Venice. It was Eugène the Count rather than Eugène the Christian who possessed control of his actions. Eugène the Count did not know what was best; he lived not for the glory of God, but for his own.

It is unclear in what area the crisis touched Saint Eugène the most. There is reason to believe Eugène struggled with gluttony and sins of overindulgence. While praying about the need to seek out mortifications in reparation for his sins, he wrote:

> [T]his body, unworthy tool of sin, this body which has so often drawn my soul into excesses which turned it into God's irreconcilable enemy, this body, secretly groaning under the empire that the soul has re-imposed on it by God's powerful grace, indignantly refuses to become itself the instrument of its own punishment.

The spiritual crisis Eugène discussed in letters and retreat notes could have also focused on not making God a priority in his life. In the retreat notes he made just after entering the seminary, Eugène mentioned of a lack of gratitude towards God. He wrote, "I am convinced, therefore, that I never truly loved You." His 1814 retreat notes read: "While as for me, until the time of my conversion, my sole preoccupation was to destroy His work, and in this I was only too successful…Since my conversion, there has been, it is true, a certain change, but I have nothing to be complacent about in my actions." Eugène would also express regret and feel guilty because of his abandonment of his vocation.

A third theory is that Eugène's spiritual crisis centered on the desire for prestige and notoriety that had taken root in Palermo. His actions were rude,[29] haughty, self-assured, and arrogant. In Palermo, Eugène once accused Pope Pius VII of dishonoring himself by granting a plenary indulgence to the people of France without demanding full restitution of all property confiscated during the French Revolution. On another occasion, Eugène criticized the archbishop and people of Aix for being so enamored with a group of religious who had recently begun serving in the city. Of these sisters, Eugène wrote:

> [C]alled the Grey Sisters or the Table Napkin Sisters because of the rag they wear on their heads…They are all the rage. And since they have taken up residence in our city, we can no longer rely on our house servants because it is almost endemic for them to go shut themselves up, to deck themselves out in the rag that endows them with such a peculiar charm…this community is made up of scully maids and it seems logical to me that they should wear the emblem of their original profession.

It is more likely, however, that Eugène's attitude and selfish desires were merely symptoms of the larger crisis taking place within his soul. The source of the crisis was something else. The chief struggle of the crisis is difficult to know, for Eugène's tendency to the extreme leads to problems if his writings are taken too literally. One must examine his writings bearing in

---

[29] In an 1803 letter to his father, Eugène wrote: "The very next time you see the Princess of Vintimille please tell her that I wrote her two letters that seem to have been lost in the mail. It is not true, but a person has to find some excuse."

mind the personality of their author. Eugène himself wrote a disclaimer in his retreat notes discussing his spiritual crisis just in case they were confiscated and examined by someone else, specifically policemen or authorities of the French government:

> When I speak of "my crimes," this is to be taken to mean grave faults which I acknowledge I had the misfortune to commit against God in the secrecy of my conscience, so that, although it can be said in all truth that before God I am a very great sinner, I could nevertheless maintain when faced by persons for whom this language has no meaning, if I thought as they do, that I am a better man than they are, for not only have I never been guilty of theft, of murder, nor done anything in anyway wrong or harmful to anybody at all in the whole wide world, not only have I never taken anyone's wife, something at which really decent people in the world would draw the line, but in addition I have always based my beliefs and actions on this principle, that both reason and religion categorically require one to abstain from coveting what belongs to another, and never to consent to do anything with anybody at all which they could be sorry for later: in short, that I have never given any scandal of any kind nor at any period of my life. I call upon all those who have known me in every country where I have lived to confirm this.

Eugène's crimes were not legal crimes, but spiritual ones. This warning about his word choice reduces the possibilities as to what his sins were, yet it does not even come close to revealing the full extent of his betrayal of God. Eugène felt they were as serious as crimes, but this is his line of thinking. It is entirely possible that the "open defection" Eugène wrote about in his notes from multiple retreats was nothing more than simply religious apathy, an affliction as common in France at the time as it is today.

In short, specific details of his spiritual crisis will never be fully known. It is clear, though, that a crisis that continued over a period of years did occur and that during that time Eugène suffered from tepidity, grew apart from God, and fell into what he later described as "horrible, execrable mortal sin, in which for long I was happy to dwell, or to be more accurate, under whose empire I groaned for many a year."

Light Breaks Through

Friendships

Loneliness had been plaguing Saint Eugène de Mazenod since leaving Don Bartolo at the end of 1797. His spiritual crisis only intensified his feelings of being alone. After years of being without virtuous friendships, Eugène finally found the friend he desired in a doctor named Emmanuel Gaultier de Claubry whom he met in September 1805. This relationship benefitted Eugène both emotionally and spiritually and lasted until the doctor's death fifty years later. Soon, two more friends joined Eugène's circle. In the summer of 1806, Eugène reconnected with a friend from Turin, and that same year he became friends with Charles de Forbin-Janson with whom he would be classmates at Saint Sulpice Seminary. In addition to these peers, Eugène also made the acquaintance of two priests who would aid in solidifying his path in life, Father Augustin Magy and Father Antoine du Puget Duclaux.

Work in the Prison

In December of 1806, Eugène obtained a position managing the prisons in Aix. Under his guidance, many reforms were made to the prisons in Aix. These reforms focused on improving the prisoners' lives, not merely punishing them. Eugène ensured they had an acceptable quality of food and that they were kept clean by giving them a clean shirt at least once per week. The prisoners may have been given better living conditions, but the bulk of the reforms Eugène implemented focused on reforming the prisoners themselves. Eugène noted the sorry attempt the prisons were making to influence the prisoners' spiritual lives and attempted to remedy the situation by only feeding Catholic prisoners after they had attended Mass. His coworkers in the prison management system were miffed by the large number of reforms Eugène implemented, but he was not deterred by this. However, Eugène's tenure working within the prison system lasted less than a year. His resignation letter cited unspecified domestic issues that were taking up too much of his time.

1806: A Turning Point

The year of 1806 was significant in the life of Saint Eugène de Mazenod. During this year, his life began to improve, both personally and spiritually. In September, he wrote a letter to his father that displays a changed mindset:

> As to myself, it is more than likely that my father's absence has set my destiny on a course quite contrary to what the feelings of my heart, in the past so eager for glory, seemed to hold out for me. I will perhaps be all the happier for it if I am able to turn my scarcely voluntary inactivity to my heavenly profit, an inactivity that I would never have shrugged off without the advice and counsel of a father as enlightened as mine.

Eugène became able to see the good that could come from his sufferings. The separation from his father and the refusal of his parents to reunite now awakened him to the idea that the Lord had grander plans for him than he could have imagined. His sufferings allowed him to recognize that the plans of God and the plans of Eugène were not the same.

Eugène's letters from seminary indicate that his spiritual life was renewed in 1806,[30] and it is certain that by Christmas of 1806 his call to the priesthood had been reawakened.[31] Years later, he wrote of the Lord calling him back to a deeper spiritual life:

> This generous Prince watched out to save me, He ambushed me at the moment my thoughts were far from Him, and binding me once again more by the bonds of His love than those of His justice, He brought me back to His camp. Yet again, I had escaped Him, blind fool that I was. But this time it was for ever, for ever! May the memory of my revolt perish.

Eugène's words above mention the Lord's love for him, not His wrath as the main reason for the conversion. However, typical of his character, in his later retreat notes, Eugène over-emphasized his faults during his crisis and barely mentioned the spiritual graces he received when he began to embrace the love of the Lord again. Therefore, like his spiritual crisis, little is known about the specific details of his conversion.

The Nature of His Conversion

The exact nature of Saint Eugène's conversion and the motives behind it are unknown. It is known, however, that Eugène did not convert out of fear of Hell. "I have never needed

---

[30] Of this time period, Eugène wrote to his mother, "You must have noticed yourself that I had begun to come out of that state of tepidity into which I had fallen, and which infallibly would have led to death."

[31] A letter Eugène wrote to his mother in 1809 mentioned that he would be ordained to the sub-diaconate around Christmas of that year. At that point he would have been discerning the priesthood for three years.

the idea of Hell to bring me to God; I have never been able to bring myself to dwell on it in my acts of contrition," he once wrote. "When I ignored God, fear of Hell did not hold me; now that I have come back to Him (by a quite different road than fear of Hell), even were there no Hell, I would want to love my God and serve Him all my life." It was, not fear of eternal damnation, but the love of God that pulled Eugène out of his spiritual tepidity. His 1814 retreat notes shed some light on the nature of his conversion:

> I stayed most with the following thoughts: that God created me, and indeed could only have created me for Himself, that He fashioned me according to His designs to make use of me in what He knew would contribute to His Glory and procure my salvation. While as for me, until the time of my conversion, my sole preoccupation was to destroy His work, and in this I was only too successful…Since my conversion there has been, it is true, a certain change, but I have nothing to be complacent about in my actions.

Eugène mentions a meditation on an idea. This suggests Eugène, dissatisfied with how his life had turned out thus far, began pondering why God created him. The answer he found led to his conversion. Eugène never claimed to have reasoned his way to a conversion, but given the statement above, it would be a logical conclusion.

"One Good Friday…"

While he was emerging from his spiritual crisis, Eugène de Mazenod attended a Good Friday[32] service that would change

---

[32] Historians have debated the year in which this event took place. The year 1807 is the most popular choice, but 1806 has its supporters as well. However, the actual date is unknown and will never be known. Saint Eugène only mentioned this event one

his life. He had been struggling with his guilt over spending years in what he described as habitual mortal sin. Yet, on the day the Church remembered the death of Jesus Christ, he found himself struck by the Lord's love and mercy. It was a moment that he would never forget. Years later, Eugène wrote of the experience:

> I looked for happiness outside of God and, to my sorrow, looked there for too long a time. How many times, in my past life, did my heart, torn, tormented, throw itself in desperation at its God whom it had abandoned? Can I ever forget those bitter tears which the sight of the Cross caused to stream from my eyes one Good Friday? Ah! They welled up from the depths of my heart and nothing could stop them. They were too abundant to hide from the people who, like myself, were attending that moving service. I was in mortal sin, and it was this that caused my sorrow. It was a moment singularly different from what I had experienced in certain other instances. Never was my soul more relieved, and never did it feel happier. And it was simply because, during that torrent of tears, despite my grief, or better, by reason of it, my soul leapt toward its final end, toward God, its only good, whose loss it felt so keenly. Why say more? Could I ever do justice describing what I felt at that moment? Just thinking about it fills my heart with sweet consolation.

---

time years later and did not record when it occurred other than Good Friday. Any statement as to the actual year of this experience is merely conjecture and should be treated as such. There is no reason to make a conjecture because the year is not important. This event was not the beginning of Eugène's conversion, nor was it the final crescendo. This spiritual experience was one part of a larger movement within Eugène's soul.

Thus, I looked for happiness outside of God, and outside of him found only affliction and misfortune. But happily—happily a thousand times over—that good Father, despite my unworthiness, showered me with the riches of his mercy. The least I can do now is make up for lost time and redouble my love for him. Let all my actions, thoughts, etc., be directed toward that end. What more glorious occupation than, in all and for all, to act only for God, to love him above all, to love him all the more because I have come to love him so late. Ah! The happiness of Heaven begins here below....Let us choose now!

Although it was mentioned just one, brief time in his writings, the way Saint Eugène de Mazenod describes it reveals the profound effect this spiritual experience had on him. This moment has been discussed in detail in biographies about Eugène de Mazenod, and each author has his own opinion of the event's significance. It was a major spiritual experience in Eugène's life, one of tremendous grace, and it would not be too bold to conjecture that this experience aided in pulling Eugène out of a spiritual hole and thrusting him into deeper intimacy with the Lord, as well as helping solidify his vocation, even though he would not enter the seminary until more than a year later.

One thing is clear, though: Through the grace of this experience, God took Eugène's sorrow over his sins and turned it into joy. This grace-filled moment, at a time in his life when he needed it the most, drew Eugène into a deeper intimacy with the Lord and helped him to understand his identity in God's eyes. He had been struggling emotionally and spiritually, grasping for some sense of meaning and purpose in his life, and then the Lord broke through to fill his soul with peace and joy. These graces, received at the foot of the Cross, created a mindset within Eugène where he felt compelled to respond to the great love the Lord had for him with total obedience to the Lord's will for his life.

Following the Call

Solidifying the Vocation

As the fog of his interior struggle was dissipating, Eugène befriended an elderly priest, Father Augustin Magy, a priest in his eighties, living out the final years of a life dedicated to the Lord. Many had sought his wisdom, but none had captured his attention quite like the young man in his twenties who came seeking guidance and instruction. The elderly prelate picked up where Don Bartolo Zinelli had left off in schooling Eugène in Ignatian spirituality. Despite the approximately sixty-year age gap, Magy and Eugène grew close. It is entirely possible Eugène was closer to Father Magy than he was to his own family.

Throughout the course of his friendship with Magy, Eugène had been flirting with the idea of becoming a priest. The wise priest helped steer the young man into a prayer life capable of understanding the Lord's will for his life. Perhaps, Father Magy's patience ran out, or perhaps, he felt he could no longer remain idle while Eugène hesitated to follow the tremendous plan the Lord had for him.[33] Whatever the reason, he ceased

---

[33] Father Magy predicted Eugène's canonization. He wrote to Eugène, "You have a devotion to Saint Ignatius. That great saint trained so many apostles. He will obtain for you the grace to be one. You, you will be one. I have the feeling you will be…You have the desire to be a martyr; that is the desire characteristic of an apostle."

trying to steer Eugène and bluntly told him, "[Y]our vocation is as certain as it can be, that's all you have to know." Father Augustin Magy also stated that he would die happy if he knew that a young man of the character of Saint Eugène de Mazenod was entering the priesthood around the same time his priesthood was ending. He felt honored to have Eugène replace him.

In addition to Father Magy, Eugène also sought the wisdom of Father Antoine du Puget Duclaux who had an international reputation as a spiritual director. Eugène himself believed Duclaux to be the best director of conscience in all of France. Just before committing himself to the priesthood, Eugène visited him in Paris to share with him his thoughts about the priesthood and to ask if it was the right thing to do. The answer from Father Duclaux, who would later be his spiritual director at Saint Sulpice Seminary, was whole-heartedly in the affirmative.

Interior Impediments

Because of the lengthy interior struggle he experienced, Eugène felt there were interior impediments to pursuing a priestly vocation. In a letter he wrote to his friend Emmanuel Gaultier de Claubry, he expressed these concerns:

> And now, shall I speak of myself? Yes, but only to ask for your prayers, to give you the charge expressly to persevere in asking God to accomplish in my regard the adorable designs whose outcome I impede by my infidelities; that He might knock, prune, reduce me to desiring only what He wills, that He might overturn all the obstacles standing in the way of my arriving at a more perfect state to which I strongly believe I am called. May He give me the grace of recognizing ever more clearly the vanities of this miserable earth, so that I see only those heavenly goods that the moth cannot corrupt. In a word, may He make me worthy of the Communion of Saints and have me assume the place

among them that He seems to have destined me for, but which it seems to me I am still far from deserving.

Eugène's years of "open defection" created a comfortability with sin. He worried that his attachment to sin would prevent him from following the Lord's call. The interior chaos created by his spiritual crisis concerned him. Eugène knew the priesthood was a sublime calling, and he wanted to be worthy of it. So, despite knowing in his heart and from the mouths of two wise priests that he was destined for the priesthood, Eugène still felt trepidation about pursuing his vocation.

His Mother's Reaction to His Vocation

Marie-Rose Joannis had plans for her son's life, but Eugène de Mazenod was being drawn away from that path. He rediscovered the calling he had first felt in Venice while being tutored by Don Bartolo Zinelli. Eugène knew it was his duty to follow the will of God, but he also knew that following God's will would displease his mother. Therefore, it was necessary for Eugène to prepare his mother before informing her of his decision to enter the seminary. There was a need to prepare himself to answer her objections and to have others help him soften the blow.

Eugène enlisted the help of the Jansenist Roze Joannis and his sister Ninette to prepare Marie-Rose for their conversation about his vocation. Roze Joannis had tremendous influence over his cousin and would prove to be valuable in calming Marie-Rose's outrage over Eugène's decision by pointing out how happy Eugène had become since finding God's will for his life. Eugène's opponent in theological debates, who had influenced the permanent separation of his parents and the seizure of his father's property, now became his chief ally. After Roze had first broached the subject of the priesthood, Eugène brought in his sister Ninette to charm away any further misgivings Marie-Rose might still have about his vocation.

Once Roze and Ninette had finished prepping Marie-Rose, Eugène himself told his mother of the call he had heard from the Lord:

> As the Lord is my witness, what He wants of me is that I renounce a world where it is almost impossible to find salvation, such is the power of apostasy there; that I devote myself especially to His service and try to reawaken the faith that is becoming extinct amongst the poor; in a word, that I make myself available to carry out any orders He may wish to give me for His glory and the salvation of souls He has redeemed by His precious Blood.

After his initial declaration to his mother, Eugène continued to explain his reasoning to her through several letters, most of which were written after he entered the seminary. He desired to banish any fears his mother might have, to remind her that all are obligated to follow God's will, to assure her that he would always be attached to his family, and to make her fully understand why he was giving his life to the Church.

Eugène called upon his mother's belief in God and that He has a plan for everyone. "He has graciously willed to call me to so high an honor by a vocation which so obviously comes from Him," he wrote to her. He stressed the importance of following God's will, telling her, "[W]e must follow it and count ourselves very fortunate, even offering unceasing thanksgivings when he calls us to the greatest thing on earth and in heaven." To Eugène, it was the duty[34] of each person to submit to "the Master's designs we are all bound to obey on pain of damnation."

Not only did Eugène feel his call was an obligation, but he also felt it was a gift: "The grace of vocation to the clerical state

---

[34] Shirking one's duty was unthinkable to Eugène who once wrote, "Death, and I mean this literally, death should seem preferable to me to transgressing an important duty."

is not given to everybody and that is something that should make those of us appreciate it all the more whom God's mercy calls to share his sufferings and the sublime ministry of the God-Man." He was honored to be called to the priesthood and felt his mother should be honored to give her son to God's service.

Furthermore, Eugène hoped to draw his mother's attention to the good her son could do as a priest. He told his mother that he was becoming a priest to save souls. "Dear mother, if you really grasped a great truth, that souls ransomed by the Man-God's blood are so precious that, even if every human being, past, present, and to come, were…to save just one single one… it would still be time well, nay admirably well spent," he wrote to her. In addition to the salvation of souls, Eugène reminded his mother of the Church's great need for priests:

> As you see, the ranks are getting thinner every day, soon the Church will be at a loss to know to whom she might confide her children, and one would have to be slothful indeed not to burn with the desire to come to the aid of this good Mother in her well-nigh desperate plight. Does not the fact of feeling this desire vividly, deeply rooted in the heart, in these unhappy times when the faith produces but faded fruits, in itself offer a clear sign of the will of the sovereign mover of hearts? However, it is not for us to assert this.

Eugène's desire to see the Church blessed with high-quality priests was a significant motivating factor for Eugène's decision to become a priest, for he cited this same reason when he explained his vocation to his father: "[A]fter 25 years, [the Church] could no longer confide the divine ministry, which before had been sought after by the highest in the land, to any but poor workers, wretched peasants." This statement, while exhibiting his still-present class consciousness, displays the great love Eugène had for the Church and his desire to see it flourish.

Despite Eugène's conviction of his calling and his demonstration of the need for priests, Marie-Rose continued to hold on to a dream to see him find financial comfort through marriage, but no earthly concern could shake Eugène's belief that he was called to something greater. He despised the pleasures of this world and abhorred the idea of pursuing them any further. "Haven't I already given too much of my time to this world, when I should rather have been at war with it, enemy as it is to Jesus Christ?" he wrote. "And when this divine Master calls me to Him to serve His Church, at a time when she is abandoned by everyone, am I to resist his voice and pine away in an alien land?" He pointed out to her that if he married and had children he would have less time to spend with her than if he were to become a priest. Eugène, once again, declared his distaste for marriage:

> No thank you very much, I have such an aversion and distaste for marriage that the very idea makes me ill; I would sooner spend my life in the hulks (galleys). But it is instituted by God, sanctified by Our Lord who made it a sacrament. St. Paul says that whoever gets married does a good thing. Who denies it? Marriage is a good thing for those who are called to it; and these very people have to agree that this good thing very often gives rise to some rather bad things…For the rest, it isn't my affair, as marriage and I are at opposite poles.

Eugène's last strategy to ease his mother's concerns was to get her to imagine how wonderful it would be to have a son as a priest. "You will be besides yourself for joy, and I am quite sure tears will flow from your eyes, when you receive the precious body of Jesus Christ from the hands of your son," he wrote to her. Eugène loved his mother and desired to see her filled with joy. He thought she would find peace in the midst of her anxieties about his vocation in the image of the one, whom she had given life and nourishment from her own body, giving her spiritual life and nourishment via his ministry as a priest.[35]

A Trial Period in the Seminary

Not wanting to oppose the will of God, Marie-Rose reluctantly consented to Eugène entering the seminary in October of 1808, but only because she believed it to be a testing ground for his vocation. She did not realize how firmly the priestly vocation had been implanted in Eugène's mind and soul. In her mind, Eugène's entrance into the seminary was only on a trial basis. Her worries soon increased as her son Eugène fully embraced the ecclesial life. Each step of Eugène's journey towards ordination increased Marie-Rose's sorrow. She scolded him for how soon he received the tonsure (December 17, 1808). He had only waited three months to receive the tonsure, and when she heard the news, Marie-Rose wrote, "I am in a state of fearful anxiety."

Eugène was ordained to the subdiaconate on December 23, 1809, and to the diaconate on June 16, 1810. Both ordinations filled Eugène with a joy he could not fully describe, despite his mother's reservations. On the occasion of his ordination to the subdiaconate, he wrote to his mother, "It would be impossible to try now to convey to you any idea of the joy the Lord poured into my soul that happy day." Three days after his ordination to the diaconate, Eugène wrote to his mother, "If I so much as begin talking about merely one of the joys that has captivated my heart, I shall never end this letter."

At each step of the journey to ordination, she became more and more concerned with how quickly he was progressing towards

---

[35] Following his ordination, Eugène wrote to his mother: "You gave me life and nourishment from your own body. Now I am able to give you a nourishment that my priesthood prepares for God's children, hungry for the holy bread which alone is able to give life."

ordination. In response to his ordination to the sub-diaconate, Marie-Rose told Eugène of her struggle accepting his commitment to the Church. To which he responded:

> It is not the sub-diaconate that binds me to the clerical state; it is my full, entire, voluntary and well-thought-out decision...God calls me to the clerical state. I want to be a cleric, and I want it very much. And note that I don't want to be a cleric for eight days, six months, a year, ten years even; I want to be one for the whole of my life. Now, for that, I must be tonsured, porter, lector, exorcist, acolyte, sub-deacon, deacon, priest; these are conditions necessary to attain my end.

Eugène wanted to be firm in his conviction that he was called to be a priest, but he also wanted his mother to be free from anxiety. His responses to his mother's worries always reiterated that he was following God's will and that he loved her:

> Do you believe that a man strongly moved by God's spirit to imitate Jesus Christ in His active life...Do you believe, I say, that such a man who had a clear vision of the needs of the Church and who, despite the attraction God gives him to work at helping her, and other signs of His will, yet opted to sit back with arms folded, sighing softly to himself about all these evils, but not raising a finger to awaken even in the least degree man's hardened hearts, would rest in all good conscience? What an illusion! Once again, one can sanctify oneself only in the place where God wants us to be...No decision was ever more carefully and lengthily discussed than the one I am taking...Ah, my God! If the Lord had not inspired this resolution, could I have endured even the thought of causing you to shed one single tear? Answer me that, knowing my heart as you do.

Purgation

God's Mercy

God called Eugène de Mazenod to be a priest, despite the fact that he struggled with sin for years. Eugène felt immense gratitude for the mercy he received from the Lord. During his first days of seminary, he wrote:

> The soul is great, it can embrace an abundance of objects, it can be moved simultaneously by a diversity of feelings. And so without gainsaying the feelings of sorrow, and at the same time of utter trust in God's mercy, it must also be employed in the thanksgiving it owes to this good Father for the signal favors He has generously wished to grant it. It must bless Him every moment of the day for having generously willed to cast a merciful glance upon it, one of His powerful glances that do such great things; it must offer itself every day as a holocaust to thank Him for snatching him from the hands of the devil, from the jaws of Hell, it must be melted, emptied, at the thought that not only has this excellent, rich, generous Master displayed His power on its behalf to withdraw it from vice, but He has willed to choose for it a home, to call it to a state which, in bringing it close to Jesus Christ, places it in the happy necessity of centering its thoughts solely on this divine Savior, of serving Him with more ardor, loving Him without cease.

Eugène was awestruck at the supreme goodness of the Lord's mercy. He had done nothing to merit forgiveness, yet God had granted it to him anyway. While on retreat in 1809, Eugène wrote, "When I look back over my past life, I see only disorder, iniquity on my side, a pouring out of graces on God's side. The most signal of all these is to have pulled me back from the gutter to set me at the foot of His throne in His sanctuary." Eugène pulled away from God, but the Lord pursued him despite his betrayal. For years, he marveled at the Lord's goodness and persistence:

> This soul that You gave me to praise you, bless You, love You with, defied You, insulted Your generosity, turned from You and plunged into the filthy mire, from whence perhaps she would never have emerged, if, to crown all Your mercies towards me, You had not worked some miracles in my favor.

> You never ceased to speak to me in my heart, which was hard and insensitive only towards You. The further I distanced myself from You, the closer You pressed at my heels. You were the tender and dear Father who does not cease to support and embrace His well-beloved son who grows angry in his frenzy against the benevolent hand which he fails to recognize, as he has lost the use of reason.

Eugène marveled at the relentless pursuit the Lord undertook for His lost sheep. These writings reveal the wisdom Eugène had with regards to understanding that he could not make sense of his Creator's mercy. He also felt the Lord extended more mercy towards him than He had towards others:

> I thought of God as doing for me much more than He had done for others; gratitude filled me as I admired the wholly merciful plan He has followed in my regard, and my gratitude grew all the more when I considered that my

innumerable infidelities have not deflected Him at all from these merciful plans for me…He put up with me, He affected not to see the damnable injuries that I continually inflicted on Him; never changing, He opened to me His loving heart. Monster that I was, instead of hastening to consume within it all my crimes, I cruelly wounded it; and still God offered it to me full of love, ready to receive me, urging me to enter, etc. How long did it last, this prodigious scene of love on the one hand, of barbarity, folly on the other?

Even so, God having kept to His plan, having so to speak pursued me until He recaptured me, me the black sheep, me the disgusting leper…I had to conclude that God has some special plan for me, that He has some plan for me for His glory.

But could it be possible that after seeking me for so long when I was fleeing from You, You would no longer want me when I came back? I am too happy, Lord, that You would really want to furnish me the means to do something for Your glory in reparation for the outrages I have done for so long a time.

Eugène predicted that the Lord had grand plans for him, a prediction that would later prove true. With his suspicion of a grand plan at work, Eugène knew there would be no escaping God's will. Yet, grateful for the mercy bestowed upon him, he still felt unworthy of his call to the priesthood. Eugène knew his past sins left wounds that still needed healing and that his passionate personality needed taming.

The Need to Purge

Shortly after his entrance into Saint Sulpice Seminary on October 12, 1808,[36] Saint Eugène de Mazenod wrote the following self-portrait for Father Duclaux:[37]

> I am a lively and impetuous type of character. When I want something I want it very badly, I am impatient of the least hold up and I find delays unbearable. Firm in my resolutions, I chafe against anything that gets in the way of carrying them out, and I would not let anything stand in my way to overcome even the most difficult obstacle. Obstinate in my desires and feelings, I rebel at the mere hint of opposition; if it persists and unless I am really sure that I am being opposed for a higher good, I become heated and then I find within myself new and hitherto unknown resources, I mean I acquire all of a sudden a remarkable fluency in the expression of my ideas which come all in a rush, although in my normal state I often have to dig for them, and express them but slowly. I experience the same facility when I am deeply moved by anything and really want others to share my feelings.

The self-description above does not describe the stereotype of a saint. Yet, those were the words twenty-six-year-old Eugène

---

[36] The date of Saint Eugène's entrance into the seminary is significant because it is before his sister's wedding. He knew prior to his entrance that she was about to be married, but he felt so strongly about his vocation that he decided to forgo attending the wedding of his sister to Marquis Armand de Boisgelin on November 21, 1808.

[37] Oblate historian-theologian J. Pielorsz notes that the calm demeanor and wisdom of Father Duclaux helped Saint Eugène de Mazenod control his haughty, passionate, and class-conscious personality.

de Mazenod used to describe his personality, a personality he knew he needed to tame to prepare for his ordination to the priesthood. Moreover, the class-consciousness that implanted itself in his brain early in his life and grew roots during his stay in Palermo remained present in his mind.[38] He needed to rid himself of this mindset in order to be a holy priest. Despite his conversion prior to entering the seminary, Eugène recognized imperfections still lingered in his soul. It was not enough to have to resolve to never sin. He desired to purge all attachment to sin:

> There is no question of speaking here of what is against God's law, the mere fact of crossing the threshold of the seminary is a proof of the resolution made never to commit a mortal sin and of one's horror at anything that might wound in its essence the divine majesty. "Nothing against God" is the wholly indispensable watchword of every Christian however feeble his fervor; a man aspiring to the clerical state must go infinitely further. Horror then, the greatest horror before

---

[38] Eugène's assertion that the Church was in dire need of priests was not only inspired by the shortage of priests, but also by the people who were being ordained to the priesthood. This is evident by statements he made in his writings during this period of his life such as "the priestly character of Jesus Christ's ministers could naturally command respect in view of their education and birth," and "in my position, as I have said many times before, I am obliged to be better instructed than most others." It should be noted that, at this time in history, the Church in France did not offer pleasant prospects for their potential priests. At any moment, the political climate could shift in a direction that would place the lives of priests in danger. Therefore, those who entered the priesthood at this point in France's history most likely had a definite call from God. Eugène's concern over the quality of French priests were probably exaggerated at best.

anything that might be an offense to God in His goodness. But more, I must tie myself down to the most scrupulous fidelity in even the smallest things…Could I ever have any doubt about my very great need of penance? It is my fond hope (and this is the source of my strength) that Our Lord Jesus Christ has restored me to His good graces by ratifying the sentence of absolution given me when contrite and humbled I confessed the sins of my whole life, but I know full well that this very fact of absolution from guilt leaves me to expiate and cancel out the punishment, and must I not be fully convinced that in the light of the enormity and number of my faults, this expiation must be the business and occupation of my whole life.

In the above retreat notes, Eugène expresses an understanding of the need for penance and purgation. There is also present a sense that Eugène felt his ministry as a priest would help atone for the sins he committed. In short, Eugène felt his sins were so great that it would take a long time to mitigate the remnants of his sinful past. Only the Lord knows how much temporal punishment was due to Eugène for his sins, but in Eugène's mind, there was much for which to atone.

It would not be easy to return to sanctity for Saint Eugène, for he faced resistance from the Evil One and his own body. "The means I use to go to God are often the very weapons [demons] use to fight me with, the society of saints, the temple of the Most High, spiritual reading, prayer," he wrote, "nothing is sacred to them, everything serves as a battle ground, in a word, it is one continual assault. One must fight from dawn to dusk." Aside from temptation from without, Eugène knew temptations would come from within, for his body's natural inclination was to reject mortification and other difficult means of sanctifying oneself.

The Purge

Eugène recognized that his initial conversion was not sufficient for establishing a habit of sanctity. He needed to refocus his "thoughts solely on this divine Savior, of serving Him with more ardor, loving Him without cease."[39] In Eugène's mind, he needed to be free of attachments to sin before he could find happiness. "My soul, an emanation from the divinity," he wrote, "will only be perfectly happy when, freed from worldly hindrances, it can occupy itself in the contemplation of its Creator."

The resolutions Eugène made upon entering the seminary were focused on the Sacraments and mortification. He received Communion three times per week and went to Confession once per week. Inspired once again by Saint Aloysius Gonzaga, Eugène's mortifications[40] consisted of fasting a total of 120 days per year (twice the number required at the time),[41] limiting the amount of food he ate on a daily basis,[42] and heating his room as little as possible during the winter.[43] Eugène maintained this practice of denying himself as best as he could. The subconscious signals he received from his body occasionally made him relax his practices. Whenever Eugène noticed his laxity, he responded by renewing his self-sacrifices with fervor.

---

[39] From his retreat notes of October 1809.

[40] Eugène attempted to add waking up an hour early to his mortifications, but his superiors and a doctor mandated that he stay in bed as long as everyone else in order to get seven hours of sleep.

[41] His list of days of fasting was approved by his spiritual director.

[42] Father Duclaux intervened and made him increase his food intake, especially during Lent when Eugène ate as little as possible.

[43] If left to his own devices, Eugène would not have heated his room at all, but his wise superiors intervened again and forced him to heat his room which reached temperatures as low as ten degrees. Eugène said to his mother who was worried about him and his behavior, "Just think of all the money I am saving you!"

In a spirit of sacrifice and expiation, Eugène maintained a simple lifestyle in the seminary.[44] His room was sparsely furnished, and his clothes were simple.[45] He wore no jewelry to decorate his body, referring to it as "useless adornment." No longer did Eugène have any concerns about maintaining the country estate in Saint Laurent, calling it "[j]ust a heap of stones." Furthermore, he refused to hire someone to clean his room, a task he previously would have seen as beneath him. These sacrifices were designed as reparation for his previous sins and to tame his personality and class consciousness. Eugène was pleased by the lifestyle he was now leading and renounced all of his previous desires for wealth and nobility. He felt called to serve the poor in his priestly ministry and desired a lifestyle fit for that goal, a lifestyle he managed to maintain for the remainder of his life.

It cannot be said, however, that Eugène sought to torture himself, nor is it true that he blamed his body for his past

---

[44] During his first retreat as a seminarian, Eugène wrote, "To punish myself for the creature comforts I overindulged in in the world, and the kind of fondness I had for certain vanities, I shall observe poverty in my cell, and live simply outside it. I will do without a fire so far as I can without excessive discomfort, I will see to my own needs, sweep my room, etc."

[45] On the subject of how a cleric ought to dress, Eugène said, "An ordinary soutane, woolen cincture, hair uncurled, this is and always will be the way Father de Mazenod will dress. I really don't know what people think they are achieving when they are forever adorning and pampering this wretched carcass that is destined to be food for the worms and is never less manageable than when it is treated gently. But what is pitiable in the case of people in general is shocking in a minister of the Cross. A sensual priest is in my eyes a deformed monstrosity, to be pointed out in the street, but it is all too true that you would often need more than ten fingers to do it."

failings. Eugène approached his sacrifices with the mindset of taming his spirit:

> To follow the advice of Saint Francis of Sales who says somewhere that one must not over-emphasize the punishment of the body, a poor donkey which does not bear all the blame, I will try above all to mortify my spirit, to stifle disorderly desires of my heart, bring this will of mine into submission; I will do all I can to overcome my temperament, to this end I will make use of every occasion that presents itself, and they will surely not be lacking. I will not forget, that being proud through and through, my sole concern will be to subdue it…Humility, above all humility, must be the foundation of the building of my salvation.

In addition to his mortifications and humility, Eugène sought to bring God into his everyday life. He made use of frequent ejaculatory prayers. Whenever the clock chimed or whenever someone knocked at the door, Eugène brought his mind to God. Periodically, he would stop in the chapel to simply say hello to God or look through the window of his room to catch a glimpse of the sanctuary light.

Progress or Lack Thereof

At the end of his first year in the seminary, Eugène felt dismayed at how little progress he had made:

> It isn't hard to see that I have made absolutely no progress in piety since I entered the seminary; it will not be difficult either to uncover the origin of this very deplorable disorder. It comes undeniably from a lack of a spirit of interior recollection. That is the fundamental vice, the blight that gnaws at the bit of good in all my actions so that it is true to say that I find myself at this moment bereft of good works and

that I must reckon as naught everything I have done up to the present because I did it badly.

The reader of Saint Eugène's words must once again bear in mind the personality of the writer. It cannot be said that Eugène made no progress in the spiritual life during his first year at Saint Sulpice, but it is clear that Eugène was frustrated with how little progress he had made. Furthermore, his personality drove him to push himself harder than prudence would allow, and his initial fervor waned, causing him to relax his pious practices.

However, a change did occur within Eugène during his time in seminary. His spiritual practices and mortifications were initially done out of repentance for his sins, but by the end of his time in seminary, his spiritual habits were motivated by his love for God.

Taming His Heart

Eugène's passionate personality inspired in him a deep love for family. He needed to exercise restraint, though, because he desired his heart to be free enough to give the necessary love and devotion to God. To his mother, Eugène wrote:

> You know my heart all too well, since it was formed by your own, so you will have a very clear understanding that it is as active and goes through the same feelings as your own. So we have to strive, each one of us alike, not to stifle it, which God does not want, but to hold it in check, so to speak. Scarcely a day has passed since I left you that I have not had to take myself to task for being too indulgent towards it; it is clear that it becomes a real temptation, since it afflicts and excessively saddens the soul that should enjoy unfailing peace. For the rest, it is an evil that I must bear with patiently, as it does not seem likely to ever go away. As well as that,

I like it so much that I am really afraid that the doctor may not agree with the patient.

Once again, it is difficult to separate fact from exaggeration in Saint Eugène's writing. Eugène loved his family, but we see above that he knew he had a tendency to get carried away. To avoid this, he informed his mother they needed to be careful not to become so preoccupied with one another that they flirt with idolatry. It is entirely possible Eugène's desire to love God with all his heart made him wary of giving too much affection to others, particularly his family, despite there being no real danger of falling into sin.

Virtue in the Seminary

Sound Judgement

While the need for purgation was real, it should not be assumed that there were no good qualities in Eugène de Mazenod when he entered Saint Sulpice Seminary. Eugène states in a letter to his mother that he was blessed with "quite good judgment." This proclamation of excellent judgement is another example of the arrogance that needed purging. Eugène's "quite good judgement" did not help him see the errors in the literature he was reading in the wake of Duchess Cannizzaro's death. Although, grief can weaken one's ability to properly reason. Nevertheless, there is evidence to support Eugène's claim of good judgement.

In August of 1809, Eugène and a classmate traveled to a village where some alleged seers lived. These individuals reportedly spoke with their guardian angels every night and saw other visions. Eugène reports that he had gone on a whim to visit these people, but was glad he did go. Shortly after arriving, it became clear to Eugène that the alleged seers were frauds, and he was able to convince his companion, the local parish priest, and several other individuals that those people were frauds.

Embracing the Ecclesial Life

Despite the large amount of mortifications he undertook in the seminary, Eugène did not find himself in a perpetual state of sorrow and pain. Rather, he felt great joy. Knowing he was following the Lord's will gave him peace and happiness. Eugène did all he could to embrace the clerical lifestyle, including petitioning to receive an assignment at Holy Week liturgies reserved for those further along in their journey to ordination, a petition that was granted.

Eugène's joy was contagious. In fact, it was so infectious that he found himself the target of intense anger of a family who thought he had convinced their son to enter the seminary instead of accepting his army commission. In Eugène's words:

> Magalon comes to see me almost every day, and I do not hesitate to give up my recreations for him as good comes from our conversations. The first we had together had a singular effect on him that I had neither foreseen nor desired, as enthusiasm is not something that appeals to me, even when its object is a good one, when it does not produce lasting fruits. Imagine, he got so worked up that he wrote immediately to tell his mother that, after a long conversation he had with me, he foresaw too many dangers in taking up a career in the army (he had only just obtained a commission), that he felt powerful religious feelings reawakening in his heart and a powerful desire to enter the clerical state. You can imagine how that letter would have gone down in the family, which is pinning great hopes on this young man's success as a soldier. You can understand they will be ready to crucify me. I had a chuckle over this, imagining the friends coming together to find a way to keep the young man away from a fanatic like me. In any case, they did not have to put themselves to the trouble. A single night was enough to pierce these fogs, and our young hero reverted to a plan more suited to him, namely, to take the decision to serve God as a soldier. The happiness he had seen in me had for a moment tempted him and perhaps the lively way I expressed my vivid feelings swept him off his

feet without my even trying. So his family will be wrong to imagine I tried to snatch him from them.

While Paul de Magalon did not enter the seminary at that time because of the influence of Saint Eugène de Mazenod, he did later find himself influenced by Eugène. Mazenodian biographer Yvonn Beaudoin reports that Magalon later became a member of Eugène's youth group in Aix and spent time as a postulant in the religious order founded by Eugène before ultimately becoming a brother of the Hospitaller Order of Saint John of God.

The Secret Club

In the seminary, Eugène became a member of a secret club[46] dedicated to clandestinely improving the fervor of all seminarians.[47] Eugène quickly ascended into a position of power within this club. Early on during his time in a leadership position, Eugène scolded the members of the group for not being zealous enough, a criticism that was well received. This lecture may have saved the group from dying out and inspired the group to give him even more leadership within their association.

For an example of how the secret club went about increasing the fervor within Saint Sulpice Seminary, Eugène described in a letter to his mother one endeavor he initiated:

> About a dozen of us got together and, in keeping with the mind of the Church and in order to make reparation, in so far as we can, for all the excesses contrary to the holy virtue of temperance, and others besides, during these days

---

[46] Eugène was probably drawn to the club due to its similarity with the Aa, a society within the Jesuits whom he had grown to admire during his time with Don Bartolo Zinelli in Venice.

[47] This group also had a special devotion to the Sacred Heart of Jesus and the Immaculate Heart of Mary.

of lunacy, we resolved to keep the fast these three days and offer a little expiatory prayer before the Blessed Sacrament. It was God in his goodness who gave me this idea, and it worked out as I had hoped. No one in the seminary knows anything about the little act of mortification our little society took on itself, and even the members of the society do not know that it was I who took the initiative. I notice that a lot of good things never get done for want of someone to make the suggestion; a lot of Christians have it in them to do all kinds of good works that they will never perhaps carry out unless they meet up with someone, who is often less perfect than they are themselves, but who invites them to get to work, with no more trouble to himself than that of making the proposal.

Little else is known about the activities of Eugène de Mazenod in this secret society. However, it would have a profound effect on him. After ordination, Eugène kept an eye on its activities and encouraged the founding of a similar group in the seminary in Aix. The rule of life of the society (which he helped reform) would influence the rule of life he would later compose for the Missionary Oblates of Mary Immaculate.

The Family Spiritual Advisor

During his time in the seminary, Eugène began advising his mother and sister on spiritual matters. No one in the family consciously chose that arrangement, but Eugène fell into this role out of love for them and out of concern for their souls. His letters to them, aside from giving them details of his daily life, advised on how to grow closer to God.

"Can you not hear this Savior, who calls to you from His tabernacle?" Eugène asked his mother in one letter. To his sister, Eugène wrote, "When one has faith and even a tiny modicum of love of God, it is easy to find ways of not losing sight for too long of one's well-beloved. In this way, one will find we have acquired a treasury of merits right there where unhappily every day others are losing their souls." The young seminarian burned with a desire to increase his family's faith and devotion to God. When Ninette attended parties with her husband, both she and Eugène worried about her being caught up in the immorality occurring around her. He advised her to seek the intercession of her guardian angel.[48] Above all, he encouraged the frequent reception of the Sacraments:

> You have distanced yourself from the source of graces at the very moment you most have need of them; you have refused the bread at the moment His viaticum was most necessary, you have refused the walking stick when your legs were getting weak.
>
> My child, you have spent three whole months without the nourishment of the flesh of Jesus Christ, without slaking your thirst with His precious Blood, although you should never let a single week go by without strengthening yourself with this Heavenly food. Since when has it been the practice to disarm oneself at the approach of the enemy? Tell me then whose help it is you dare to count on amidst the dangers of the world when you refuse your soul Him who is our strength and our life? Have you forgotten the anathema aimed by Jesus Christ precisely against those who, whether as an insulting gesture or from a misunderstood humility, do not participate in His Body as often as the symbols under which He hides Himself seem to invite? "If you do not eat the flesh of the Son of Man, you will not have life in you."…that is to say our soul, fainting for want of food, will lose all the strength and vigor that it can draw only from the author of life, and will succumb to an incurable

---

[48] The prayer Eugène wrote for Ninette to use in those moments can be found in the Appendix.

languor resulting in death as it opens the door to sin....I am...asking God...that He make you feel the need to yield to the arguments that my zeal for your salvation compels me to expound, or rather the holy resolution to put into practice my counsels, since I see by your letter that the arguments have already begun to have their effect.

Despite Eugène's urgings, Ninette and Marie-Rose were hesitant to frequent the Sacraments. Ninette tried frequenting the Sacraments, but saw little improvement in her spiritual life. Eugène responded to her objections by saying that no improvement was better than growing worse. Marie-Rose, on the other hand, refused to even try frequenting the Sacraments. This disappointed Eugène and inspired him to pressure her even more on the subject:

> Do you believe that there is anyone else in the world to whom your salvation, happiness, holiness are more dear than to me, or do you actually think me so blind or ignorant as to keep on proposing a means that will not be for your good? What am I to say? If I did not think it necessary for the good of your soul to frequent the Sacraments more often than you do, do you think I would keep coming back to it so often? Just remember, dear mother, that I am thirty years old, a minister of the Church, I could be a priest and I am your son, and after all that judge whether you should listen to my words. One of two possibilities must be true: either this difficulty you have about going to the Sacraments comes from yourself, or it is inspired in you by your confessor.[49] If it comes from you, it is culpable negli-

---

[49] An additional theory (which is the most likely to be correct) is Eugène's mother was influenced away from the Sacraments by her cousin and confidant Roze Joannis who wrote to Marie-Rose, "I certainly hold a high opinion of your son. He has a heart of

gence, which must at all costs be overcome. If it comes from your confessor, I do not hesitate to say in God's presence, Who hears what I say and inspires me to write these things, you must forthwith forsake this blundering guide. If everyone thought and acted in this way, Our Lord would have decided to stay with us under the species of bread all for nothing! But that is enough on that topic. Just remember that anybody who keeps from the Sacraments, either by his advice or in any other way, someone who lives as regular a life as you do, is a dangerous man from a doctrinal point of view, and one whose opinions have been rejected by the Church from apostolic times until our own.

Eugène's love for his family members inspired these lectures on the Sacraments, and it was through their shared faith and the Sacraments that he sought to mitigate the physical distance that separated them. On the day after Christmas, he wrote to his mother:

> Let us often look for one another in the Heart of our adorable Master, but above all share often in His adorable Body; it is the best way to bring us together, for, as each of us find our common identity in Jesus Christ, we become but one thing with one another. Last night, my thought was you would have wanted to honor the coming of this blessed

---

sterling quality, and that is what sets a man apart. Moreover, he is talented, has wit, is knowledgeable, has a great zeal for religion and an admirable practical piety. Among all these valuable qualities, however, he holds to some old prejudices, strengthened and increased by Sulpician teaching which can lead one far afield. It is better to be totally ignorant rather than be badly educated and ignorant of the true principles. This upsets me all the more since short of some miracle, I see no possibility for this young man to ever change his ideas."

Child, born for us, by laying Him down in your heart. As I had the same happiness at practically the same time, I united myself to you with all my soul...I was adoring Jesus Christ in my heart, I adored Him in yours, I adored Him on the altar and in the crib, I adored Him in the heights of Heaven.

Eugène did not cease encouraging his family to stay close to the Sacraments, but not all his counsels were aimed at reforming their faults. He also encouraged them to continue their virtuous habits and to pray for their brothers and sisters in Christ. He wrote in a letter to his mother:

So that is what you must do; I use such language in the name of the Church whose minister I am, but with all concern and tenderness too as your very affectionate son. Let us love Jesus, and His Church, let us believe all she teaches and condemn all she anathematizes, as she alone is infallible in her decisions. Let us pray sincerely for those led astray by pride, but let us not allow our fondness for their persons to go so far as to include their errors, which we must detest with all our strength if we wish to dwell in the barque of Peter, which is the only one that has Jesus Christ as pilot and so is the only one that can lead us to the harbor of salvation.

As Eugène prepared for the priesthood, he grew confident in the advice he was giving to his family, inspiring him to continue to offer them spiritual advice. "So in all humility I will go on as I am doing, in the hope that the Lord will give His blessing more and more to a correspondence that tends to make Him loved and served better," he wrote. Eugène, desiring to know more about the souls of his loved one's and how best to help them, encouraged them to be completely open with him. He wrote to his sister, "You must give me details, and very precise details, and especially much candor. Do not fear that I will be indiscreet." Learning about those to whom he was ministering helped him bring Christ to them in a more effective way. Eugène's desire to know the humanity of those to whom he was ministering is a precursor to the advice he gave in the initial rules he composed for the Missionary Oblates of Mary Immaculate: "We must lead men to act like human beings, first of all, and then like Christians, and, finally, we must help them to become saints."

Education

Personal Study

At the time Eugène entered the seminary, potential priests were only required to spend two years studying before ordination. The Revolution had greatly decreased the number of priests in the country, and it became necessary to ordain priests quickly. Furthermore, the priests who were ordained were not of the quality needed for the Church to flourish. The inability of many priests to give religious instruction and the effect it had on the faithful irked Eugène:

> Ignorance regarding the truths of the faith, even those necessary for salvation, was accompanied by the almost total and universal obliteration of Christian living. A scanty few still evinced in their conduct the faith practiced by our fathers. The rest lived as if the only thing that mattered was their own earthly existence and they never even suspected that something might lay beyond the confines of their narrow horizons. I make no comment on the example given them by a clergy made up of the most disparate elements… Many among them were nothing more than mercenaries; they watched over the flock to receive the wages paid them by men without any great concern for the wages awarded by God. And would that these warders, indifferent to the salvation of their flock, had not been at times wolves in the sheepfold!

Despite being convinced he was called to become a priest, Eugène stayed longer than necessary in the seminary. He knew the importance of the work he would be doing and believed he needed to be as prepared as possible. "What perhaps would be sufficient knowledge for the majority of priests would not be sufficient for me," Eugène wrote to his mother. As the son of a nobleman, he knew expectations others would have for him would be high. Eugène knew he had much to learn.

Moreover, the Revolution had limited his ability to learn the Faith as a boy, and he desired to learn all that he could before becoming a priest. In Eugène's mind, it was dangerous to send a priest into ministry before he was adequately schooled in theology and ecclesiology:

> If I want to be of some use in the ministry, I still have a lot of studying to do, and it is quite clear that I could not undertake anything in my present state and keep a perfectly clear conscience. I am well aware that there are priests who are less prepared than myself perhaps and who nevertheless press on, but it is a very great evil. And I think it is the highest form of ignorance when one thinks one knows what one is in fact ignorant of or knows only in a sketchy way.

Eugène believed that "[e]cclesiastical knowledge embraces so many subjects that no one should think it can be acquired in a hurry and, as the expression goes, on the fly." It was, therefore, necessary to spend a prolonged period of time in proper preparation for the priesthood.

Marie-Rose's Fluctuating Opinion

While attempting to purge himself of his faults and learn theology, Eugène had to endure continuous pestering from his mother about his vocation. When Marie-Rose could see that her son could not be dissuaded from his plans, she resigned herself to the fact that Eugène would become a priest. With this new mindset, she continued to pester Eugène, but now the focus was on seeing him ordained as soon as possible. Marie-Rose had come to terms with her son's plans of becoming a priest, and now she just wanted Eugène to return home to Aix and live with her. She was shocked to learn of Eugène's decision to delay his ordination. Marie-Rose, along with Roze Joannis, implored him to be ordained at the earliest possible date, but Eugène was not swayed by their views and stuck to his decision to delay his ordination in order to continue learning about the Faith.

Religious Education

One unique way Eugène was able to learn ecclesial knowledge and prepare himself for his ministry as a priest was to teach religious education classes. All of the seminarians at Saint Sulpice were required to teach catechism classes to children. Eugène was assigned to a rambunctious group of the poorest of the poor. His superiors, recognizing the undesirable nature of this assignment, assured him that this would not be his assignment for the totality of his time in the seminary. However, Eugène was thrilled with the assignment. "Rumor has it that the intention is for me to go on then to another," he wrote to his mother, "but I am not concerned with that, and I am very happy to find myself in the middle of these poor verminous lads, whom I shall try to win over to ourselves."

Eugène was successful with regards to winning over the children. He was able to control them and adequately instruct them in the Faith. Due to Eugène's success with these kids, many adults became curious enough to join the children during his classes. Years later, Eugène received a letter from one of his former students thanking him for the profound effect his teaching had on him.

This teaching experience helped Eugène learn how to preach and prepare for teaching religious education classes. In the midst of this assignment, he wrote to his mother:

> So here I am in charge of a First Communion Remedial Catechism Class…I was detailed, yesterday, Carnival Sunday, to give an instruction on the mysteries of the Trinity and the Incarnation. This instruction, that lasts about an hour, is simply a deepening of the catechism, but this deepening is quite a problem, as one has to get these abstract matters over to children and then engage them each in turn in dialogue. I find I get a lot myself out of these exercises. In the first place I get a much more precise and profound idea of the matters I have to deal with, I give them a good chew myself before passing them on to the children, I get used to public speaking, for 50 children, plus a score of curious onlookers, some of them from the house, do constitute in all reality a public; and then too I get a real insight into the method of conducting catechism classes which has enjoyed a lot of success at St. Sulpice for more than a century, with a view, God willing, to setting it up at Aix where they really have no idea what catechism is. Next Sunday, one of my colleagues will give the instruction; my job will be to give an explanation of the Gospel lasting only five or six minutes. It is a short talk that our people usually write out and learn by heart; I will go along with this practice the first few times, but later on I intend to stand less on ceremony with our children.

Saint Eugène was so enthralled with teaching that he took every opportunity he could to teach, even going so far as to create opportunities to teach. He reported to his mother that, during his summer vacation in 1810, he wanted to teach some catechism classes while visiting his grandmother. Additionally, Eugène jumped at the chance to help preach and teach at a retreat for youths. He described this in a letter to his sister:

> However, it is a real consolation to think of 7 or 800 children of all ages, for we thus designate even people 30 years

old, and a large number of relatives, spending Carnival Sunday, Monday and Tuesday doing a retreat that took up each day six or seven hours of their time. I was really happy to give them a meditation of three quarters of an hour on Our Lord's lovable qualities to bring them to a sense of how advantageous it is to follow faithfully such a good Master rather than the detestable Satan who flatters us to bring about our perdition. This edifying assembly was so well disposed, their hearts were so moved to love Him who has acquired so many rights to our gratitude and love, that everyone's tears flowed freely; I was the only one, I say it to my shame, to remain unmoved and my heart remained cold even while my spirit was penetrated with what my mouth was saying.

Even as a seminarian, it is evident Eugène had a talent for preaching that would one day earn him comparisons to Saint Ambrose.[50]

---

[50] After being compared to Saint Ambrose, Saint Eugène wrote in his journal: "I am far from being a Saint Ambrose; I am a poor sinner to whom God has given a sense of duty and whom he has called to a sublime ministry."

A Church in Need

Eugène the Spy

In 1809, Pope Pius VII excommunicated Napoleon Bonaparte for annexing the Papal States.[51] Following the excommunication, one of Napoleon's lieutenants kidnapped the Pope. It is unclear whether Bonaparte ordered the abduction of the Pope or if his lieutenant acted of his own accord. Even if the lieutenant did indeed remove the Pope from the Papal States without an order, it did not bother the self-crowned emperor that he did so. Napoleon felt certain that, with the Pope as his prisoner and with the leaders of the Catholic Church near him, he would be able to have influence over how the Church operated. Therefore, he relocated the entire College of Cardinals to Paris where it would be easier for him to meddle in Church business.

When thirteen of the cardinals resisted his campaign of influence and protested his second marriage, an enraged Napoleon banished them to various parts of his empire and confiscated their property. He also forbade them from wearing red (the color that traditionally signifies that a cleric is a cardinal). Because they were forced to wear the attire of an average parish priest, they became known as the "Black Cardinals."

---

[51] Saint Eugène de Mazenod transcribed a copy of the bull of excommunication for the rector of his seminary.

Separated from the rest of the hierarchy, the Black Cardinals needed volunteers to help them communicate with their fellow cardinals and to stay knowledgeable of the issues of the day. The task fell to a group of seminarians studying in Paris at the time. They became spies on behalf of the Church. One of these seminarians was particularly useful because he had spent over eleven years of his life living in various Italian cities and knew the Italian language well. This would not be the only time Saint Eugène de Mazenod would come to the aid of the Catholic Church; this was just one act in a clear pattern of behavior.

The Church as Mother

Eugène firmly believed that the Catholic Church ought to be viewed as a mother "who gave birth to us all in Jesus Christ." On the day of his ordination to the subdiaconate, he expressed his love and concern for Mother Church:

> How could we not but reflect with grief about her as we considered her sorrows and sufferings, how could we not be moved with sympathy for the condition of abandonment she is in?…No, no, these deeds that rend our mother have penetrated deep into our souls, and we cried out in accents of sorrow…No, no, tender dear mother, not all your children desert you in the days of your affliction; a group, small it is true, but precious for the feelings that move it, draws close around you and wipes away the tears that men's ingratitude provoke in the bitterness of your sorrow.

It pained Eugène to see his beloved Church "so terribly abandoned, scorned, trampled underfoot." Throughout his entire life, he strove to do what was necessary to assist Mother Church. Whether it was aiding the Black Cardinals or eschewing his own plans to serve the Church, Eugène did whatever he could to serve the Church and to continue the mission of her founder, Jesus Christ.

Ordination Becomes Necessary

One of Napoleon Bonaparte's fiercest opponents in the Catholic Church was the superior of Saint Sulpice Seminary, Father Jacques André Émery, who worked tirelessly to make sure the government stayed out of the affairs of the Church. It is no exaggeration to state that he worked himself to death in defense of the Church. The French government became angry and annoyed by this prelate. They worried his influence over the seminarians would poison the minds of future priests and make them resistant to any instructions they were to give the priests of the new empire. To make this pest go away, they removed him from the seminary, hoping he would cease to influence the seminarians, but Émery moved to a nearby house where he secretly directed the activities of the seminary. However, shortly after moving into this home, he died in the wake of a lengthy meeting with government officials where he vehemently defended the Pope and the Catholic Church. It would not be long before the rest of the staff was also forced out of their positions at the seminary.[52]

Napoleon's government assumed that, with no staff, Saint Sulpice Seminary would be forced to close its doors permanently and no more rebellious priests would be ordained. However, the Sulpicians foresaw their forcible exit from the seminary and had made arrangements for that eventuality. Their contingency plan involved having some of the more respectable and elder students at Saint Sulpice temporarily take over the direction of the seminary until a more permanent staff could be found. One of the seminarians chosen for the task of continuing the Sulpicians' legacy was Eugène de Mazenod who was highly respected by the now former staff of Saint Sulpice Seminary. Despite his desire to serve the poor and the most abandoned, Eugène knew

---

[52] Eugène was chosen to give a farewell address to the Sulpicians on behalf of his fellow seminarians on the day they left the seminary for the last time.

he could not refuse to come to the aid of his seminary in a time of crisis:

> I am one of the key people in the house, and in some respects, perhaps, the key person; my departure would create a scandal which could not be ignored. Whereas, the good of the house and, therefore, of the Church requires that I stay. So I will stay, for everything points to that: God's glory, the good of the Church, edification of neighbor, my own advantage.

Seeing that the Church needed him in this time of crisis, Eugène consented to being ordained, ending his self-imposed extra time of study. This decision made his family nervous, however. Previously, Marie-Rose had flipped to wanting her son ordained as soon as possible so as to have him near her again, but when the relations between the government and the Church soured, she, along with Roze Joannis and Eugène's sister, begged him to delay ordination until priests were no longer the target of persecution. Eugène responded by saying he was needed as a priest now more than ever. The danger only increased his desire to be a priest. In fact, when Eugène left Aix for Saint Sulpice Seminary in Paris, he packed a set of lay person's clothes, thinking it was entirely possible relations between the Church and the government could sour to the point where he would need to use them in order to covertly continue his studies for the priesthood. He knew his life could one day be in peril, but that did not stop him from pursuing the priesthood. Eugène was willing to give his life in service of the Church.

Ordination

Prior to his ordination, Eugène made a three-week retreat, making final spiritual preparations for the priesthood. In his retreat notes, Eugène expressed his desire to love God more and made a beautiful declaration of obedience to the Lord's will:

My God, double, triple, increase my strength a hundredfold that I may love You, not merely as much as I can, that is nothing, but that I love you as much as did the saints, as much as Your holy mother loved and loves You. My God, that is not enough, and why should I not love You as much as You love Yourself? That cannot be, I know, but to desire it is not impossible, for I form it in all sincerity in my heart, with all my soul. Yes, my God, I would like to love You as much as You love Yourself; this then is how I may undertake to make reparation for my past ingratitude…My God, that is all over henceforth and for my whole life. You, You alone will be the sole object to which will tend all my affections and my every action. To please You, act for Your glory, will be my daily task, the task of every moment of my life. I wish to live only for You, I wish to love You alone and all else in You and through You. I despise riches, I trample honors under foot; You are my all, replacing all else. My God, my love, and my all: *Deus meus et omnia*.

Solidifying his commitment to the Lord's will, Saint Eugène de Mazenod was ordained on December 21, 1811.[53] Not wanting his ordination to come at the hands of Cardinal Maury, the Gallican[54] archbishop of Paris who was only in that position because of

---

[53] Father Eugène de Mazenod celebrated his first Mass on Christmas Eve and offered the Mass for the following intentions: "To obtain forgiveness of my sins, love of God above all things, and perfect love of neighbor. Utmost sorrow for having offended such a good and lovable God. The grace of making reparation for my faults by a life wholly and solely employed in his service and for the salvation of souls. The Spirit of Jesus Christ. Final perseverance, and even martyrdom or at least death while tending victims of the plague, or any other kind of death for God's glory or the salvation of souls."

[54] Gallicanism is the belief in a limited primacy of the Pope. Gallicans accept the idea that the Pope had authority over articles of faith, but

Napoleon, Eugène traveled to Amiens to be ordained by Bishop de Mandolx, a family friend.

Following the ceremony, Eugène felt "prostrate, overwhelmed, stunned, to share…what the Lord, in His immense, incomprehensible mercy, has just accomplished in me." In a letter to his spiritual director Father Duclaux, he declared that he knew Jesus Christ better through his ordination. Eugène experienced a new intimacy with Jesus, a state which only increased his desire to save souls.

Director at Saint Sulpice

Bishop de Mandolx immediately offered to make Eugène his vicar general, an offer that Eugène rejected. Eugène had no desire for a position of prestige; his true desire was to serve the poor. Additionally, he had already committed to assisting his seminary as a spiritual director and master of ceremonies.

While on staff at Saint Sulpice Seminary, Eugène aimed to do everything with a mindset that sought "God alone, His glory, the salvation of souls, and our progress in the ways of perfection." Eugène performed his duties at Saint Sulpice Seminary admirably despite his youth and inexperience. One of the men under his care wrote him, "I will never forget the examples you have given me of a burning zeal for Jesus Christ and His worship and an absolute dedication to the Church, His Spouse and our Mother." The two traits mentioned in that testimony are traits Eugène attempted to practice throughout his entire priesthood and pass on to other priests whom he was charged with molding into better priests.

---

maintain that power of civil and temporal matters rested with the monarch/government and local bishops. Saint Eugène de Mazenod was a staunch supporter of Ultramontanism, the opposite philosophy which believes in the primacy of the Pope and rejects any interference of the government in the affairs of the Church.

Serving the Most Abandoned

Self-Sacrifice and Zeal for the Salvation of Souls

In the summer of 1808, when Eugène was first explaining his vocation to his mother, he wrote:

> What [God] wants of me is that I renounce a world where it is almost impossible to find salvation, such is the power of apostasy there; that I devote myself especially to His service and try to reawaken the faith that is becoming extinct amongst the poor; in a word, that I make myself available to carry out any orders He may wish to give me for His glory and the salvation of souls He has redeemed by His Precious Blood.

At the heart of Saint Eugène's ministry was the desire to give himself completely to the Lord and the service of the Church. He felt that ordination to the priesthood meant joining a group of "generous souls with the capacity to sacrifice their comfort and even their lives to preserve the integrity of the Faith." In order to carry out the ministry to which the Lord was calling him, Eugène was willing to suffer martyrdom. His ministry centered on self-sacrifice for the greater good. Eugène explained to his father, Charles-Antoine de Mazenod, "Pure love of the glory of God, the most ardent desire for the salvation of the neighbor, the needs of the abandoned Church, there you have the one and only reason for my entry into the clerical state." The young man who desired greatness through the nobility grew up to become a man desirous of the good of others without regard for what the consequences would be for himself.

Throughout the course of his priesthood, Eugène burned with a desire to save souls. This was the goal of all his self-sacrifices. His zeal for souls was such that he would have been satisfied if, after a lifetime of labors as a priest, he had only saved one soul.[55] The salvation of souls was the driving force of Eugène's priesthood. He was not living for himself, but for the souls God placed in his care.

Return to Aix

Newly ordained Father Eugène de Mazenod remained at his post at Saint Sulpice Seminary until October of 1812 when he felt it was appropriate to return to his hometown of Aix and begin the work to which the Lord was calling him. When Eugène returned to his hometown, Bishop Gaspard-Jean-André Jauffret, bishop of Metz and administrator of the Archdiocese of Aix, asked the new priest what type of assignment he desired. As the son of a noble family, Father de Mazenod could have requested and most likely would have received a more prominent assignment, creating a conflict between the Ancien Regime and the new state of affairs in France. Eugène instead asked to not receive an assignment at all, telling the bishop he wanted to consecrate himself to the service of the most abandoned of the city and to do so he needed to be free to act as changing circumstances demanded. The bishop agreed to the plan (no doubt, grateful to avoid a class conflict) and awarded Eugène the liberty to minister as he saw fit. The freedom awarded to Eugène (which he would later give to his oblates) allowed him

---

[55] "[I]t would be enough, if in the course of one's life, one could help even a single soul to work out his salvation to make all one's labors worthwhile," Eugène once wrote.

to improvise and to meet the needs of the people, no matter how they manifested.

Before he began his ministry, Eugène first spent several months in prayer and study. He wanted to ensure he was ready for whatever was required of him. To accomplish his goal of saving souls, Eugène needed every action to "be subordinate to what God's service and the salvation of souls requires, souls a single one of which is worth more than all the riches, honors, and temporal goods whatsoever."

Despite knowing the work he was about to begin was the Lord's will, Eugène still feared failure:

> The Church has all too much to lament in the numerous priests who bring down harm on her by their lack of awareness of the evils she suffers, who are themselves in a state of torpor and dampen down all the flames of divine love which they should be lavishing among the faithful, for whom they are the Lord's organs and instruments of His mercy. Is it my purpose to increase their number? God preserve me from such a fate. Better to die right now as I write these words.

Eugène lived in his mother's house[56] with a Trappist brother who was waiting for the reopening of his monastery. The two souls lived an essentially monastic lifestyle. They awoke at 4:30 A.M. and went to bed at 10:00 P.M., spending the entire day in prayer and study. Although he lived with his mother, Eugène refused extravagant meals or to spend time on social events. He wanted to devote himself entirely to service of the Church. In his mind, he needed to only interact with others "when God's glory or the salvation of souls requires it of me, and my door

---

[56] Eugène chose to live with his mother because she was living alone at the time. He would have preferred to live on a property his family owned in the countryside just outside of Aix, but he chose to live in the city out of concern for his mother.

will be firmly closed to everyone to whom I can be of no service," because "the life of a priest should be a life whose every day is full in the Lord's sight." Eugène resolved to focus on the Lord and doing his will, declaring, "My chief occupation will be to love Him, my chief concern to make Him loved. To this I will bend all my efforts, time, strength."

Eugène saw the Mass as the heart of a priest's duty. "Until such time as someone proves that there exists in this world an action that gives more glory to God, is more advantageous to souls, to the sanctification of the priest, the comforting of our brothers who are suffering in purgatory, I will say Mass every day," he wrote in retreat notes dated December of 1812. In taking time to further form himself and prepare for ministry, Eugène was able to better understand the mission of a priest and the centrality of the Eucharist to the Faith.

The Evangelization of the Poor

Eugène astutely recognized the failures of the current parochial model for reaching the poor and the lower classes, hence, the reason he did not want to be attached to a parish. This was the first abandoned group in society to whom he felt called to evangelize.

In his first endeavor to minister to the poor, Eugène de Mazenod presented a series of Lenten lectures to the working classes of Aix. They were offered at a time convenient for the people and were delivered in Provençal, the language of the people[57] because Eugène believed "the Gospel must be taught to all, and it must be taught in such a way as to be understood."

---

[57] Saint Eugène de Mazenod learned Provençal from his childhood nanny. However, he was not as proficient in the language as he would have liked when he began his Lenten lecture series. He even confessed this to the crowds that gathered to hear him preach on the fourth Sunday of Lent: "When we ascended this pulpit, dedicated as it is to truth, for the first time, we frankly

In his first address, on Ash Wednesday 1813, Eugène called upon the people to consider who they were in the eyes of God:

> We will begin with teaching you what you are, your noble origin, what rights it gives you, and what obligations too it imposes on you, etc.
>
> Come now and learn from us what you are in the eyes of faith.
>
> Poor of Jesus Christ, afflicted, wretched, suffering, sick, covered with sores, etc., all you whom misery oppresses, my brothers, dear brothers, respected brothers, listen to me.
>
> You are God's children, the brothers of Jesus Christ, heirs to His eternal kingdom, chosen portion of His inheritance; you are, in the words of St. Peter, a holy nation, you are kings, you are priests, you are in some way gods, *Dii estis et filii excelsi omnes*.
>
> So lift up your spirits, that your defeated souls may breathe, grovel no longer on the ground: *Dii estis et filii excelsi omnes*. (Ps. 81:6).
>
> Lift yourselves towards heaven where your minds should be set, *conversatio vestra in caelo* (Phil. 3:20), let your eyes see for once beneath the rags that cover you, there is within you an immortal soul made in the image of God whom it is destined to possess one day, a soul ransomed at the price of the Blood of Jesus Christ, more precious in the eyes of God than all earth's riches, than all the kingdoms of the earth, a

---

confessed our fears that our lack of familiarity with the Provençal language would constitute an obstacle to the fruitfulness of our instructions."

soul of which He is more jealous than of the government of the entire universe.

Christians, know then your dignity, with St. Leo I will call you sharers in the divine nature, etc.

Saint Eugène began his Lenten series by revealing to his audience that he recognized their dignity and worth. He knew he needed his audience to accept him if he was to effectively preach to them. No other preachers had ever spoken to them in this way before; it was important to let them know that he would not be like others. Eugène cared for them and desired their happiness, a happiness only found in God:

God alone was worthy of your soul. God alone could satisfy your heart. And you, in constant flight from your only good, prostituted this heart, which He gave you for loving Him, to avarice, love of pleasures; you ran in pursuit of passing creatures which all in their own way diverted you from your end by promising you the happiness that it is useless to search for outside God. The experience of your cruel errors in this matter taught you nothing and you did not become any the more percipient.

And so it is that after living 20, 30, 40 years and more without seeking God, without having God as the goal of your thoughts, action, you have wasted your whole life, merited nothing and, if you had to appear today before His fearful judgement seat, you would not have one good work to offer Him in compensation for your innumerable infidelities.

To Eugène, his audience appeared as though they had let the opinions of others affect how they perceived themselves and influence their behavior. Eugène presented to the poor of Aix a contrasting viewpoint than that which was offered to them by the rest of society. He showed them their dignity and inheritance if only they would grasp it. Eugène ended his Ash Wednesday message by reminding them what was at stake:

> After all, what is at issue here? Nothing less than salvation or the eternal loss of your souls, that is to say, the one and only thing that merits your attentions. The very thing you have given no serious thought to perhaps until this moment. It is a matter of learning what the Lord asks of you so as to procure for you an eternal happiness, what you must avoid so as not to merit a calamity that will never end.

On the fourth Sunday of Lent, Eugène preached on the Sacrament of Reconciliation continuing the themes of his Ash Wednesday sermon. He told them that, through Confession, they could reclaim their inheritance as children of God:

> From child of malediction that the sinner was, he becomes a child of God, he re-enters on all his rights to the eternal inheritance that was won for him by the Blood of the Savior. The merits he had managed to accumulate before his sin, and which would have counted for nothing if he had died in God's enmity, are returned to him again. His soul made alive by the grace of his reconciliation no longer does anything that does not have value for Heaven: a glass of cold water, the least of works done with faith and love and with still greater reason submission and resignation before all the evils that rain down on every part of this vale of tears, take on for this soul the value of degrees of glory infinite in their duration, of which God himself will be the reward.

Eugène believed that, without the Sacrament of Reconciliation, a person was a child of and a slave to sin, and he desired to see his audience receive the freedom wrought by the Lord's mercy:

> Yes, my brothers, come, and you will see with what joy we will help you to take up your yoke that will seem too heavy only for the first few moments of your conversion, for when once you are freed from sin, light will take the place of the deep shadows that reigned in your souls, God will seem so lovable to you, He will fill your hearts with so great a consolation, He will invest you with so great a strength that, like new Samsons, you will pull down with vigorous arms the gates that held you captive, and loaded with these precious spoils, you will fly to the summit of the mountain, from where you will taunt your enemies who will then seem to you as contemptible, as odious as today they seem seductive.

Knowing it is against a human being's instincts to reveal one's wrongdoings to another and that a life of sin breeds comfortability and attachment to immoral deeds, Eugène sought to ease any concerns his listeners might have about Confession and implored his audience to seek out priests who were ready to "press them close to their hearts and take delight in pouring out balm on all their wounds to ease them."

Because of the love he showed for the poorer classes, Eugène's Lenten series was well received by those for whom it was intended, and the crowds grew with each installment. Due to their unusual nature, Eugène's lectures were not only popular with the common people, but also with curious members of the middle and upper classes. All were amazed that a son of a nobleman would preach to the poor in this way.

Seminarians in Aix

During his time at Saint Sulpice, Eugène evidently developed a liking for forming future priests, for when he returned to Aix, he made it a priority to visit the seminarians who were studying in his hometown. To increase their fervor, he helped organize a group similar to the one he joined as a seminarian. Eugène knew changes were needed, and he helped fix the problems facing those in Aix's seminary. Because of his intervention, the seminary was no longer plagued by "extreme dissipation, a sovereign forgetfulness of every rule, no spirit of piety at all." Instead, the club brought about improved punctuality, increased fervor, deeper prayer, and increased frequency with which the Sacraments were received. The benefits wrought by the existence of this club delighted Eugène. When he recalled the change he witnessed in Aix's seminary, tears filled his eyes. "Nothing could be more consoling than to see how this house progresses since this useful foundation," Eugène wrote.

The Youth

Father Eugène de Mazenod felt called to serve the most abandoned of Aix, and in his zeal for the salvation of souls, he recognized the danger the youth faced. Due to the French Revolution, the teaching of the Faith had ceased, leaving the youth with no religious instruction. The children were taught instead by schools established by the government. Eugène saw these schools as Napoleon's attempt to poison the minds of the youth of France. "What he counts on most is the destruction of the moral fiber of the youth," Eugène said. "The success of the measures he has taken is frightening." The young priest believed that, by focusing on the youth, Napoleon sought to corrupt all of France by indoctrinating the country's future. In response, Eugène vowed, "I, too, will concentrate on the youth. I will make every effort to preserve the young people from the evils that are threatening them, some of which have already affected them." He could not allow himself to stand to the side and witness the poisoning of young minds.

Eugène's first step towards combatting Napoleon's scheme was to establish a sodality of young boys[58] in the hopes of forming a "corps of very pious young people."[59] This had to be done covertly, for it was illegal at the time to form groups for that purpose.

In April of 1813, Eugène visited a playground outside the city and watched some boys play. As they were about to leave, Eugène began speaking to them, and in a few short minutes, they were down on their knees praying. With this group of boys, Eugène founded the Holy Association of Christian Youth.[60]

Not everyone was allowed into the group, however, and Eugène scrutinized each applicant. He focused on finding young men who had virtuous traits that could be developed and allowed to flourish, rather than selecting children from the elite social classes, and his admissions process resembled that of a religious order. At one point of the process, the applicant

---

[58] Saint Eugène is a youth ministry hipster. He started a group for young boys twenty-eight years before Saint John Bosco (who is well known for his work forming young men) made ministering to youth cool.

[59] Quote taken from the original rules Eugène composed for his youth sodality.

[60] Two of the founding members of this group later became Oblates. Many others who joined later would also become Oblates. In fact, the first four novices to enter the religious order founded by Eugène de Mazenod were former members of the youth sodality. Ten other members of the youth sodality would follow those four into the Oblates' novitiate, three of whom persevered to become full members of the Missionary Oblates of Mary Immaculate. Other members of the sodality expressed interest in joining the Oblates, but were unable to do so. Moreover, several other youths under Eugène's care pursued vocations to the diocesan priesthood, and one became a brother of the Hospitaller Order of Saint John of God.

was required to provide a list of his friends, and once Eugène reviewed it, the boy was informed which friends he was allowed to keep and which ones he was not allowed to see anymore. If the young boy disobeyed the directive to no longer keep bad company, they were expelled from the group.

Under the leadership of Saint Eugène, the boys in the youth sodality had a strong foundation for growing in virtue and a leader capable of guiding them who had learned how to mold young boys from Monsignor Milesi and Don Bartolo Zinelli.[61] Eugène drew up for the boys a long list of strict rules and regulations for them to follow.[62] If an admitted member did not

---

[61] Many years after his time in Venice, Saint Eugène de Mazenod would continue to praise Milesi and Zinelli. In an 1842 diary entry, he wrote: "People may be surprised to hear me speak of those who took me in their care in my childhood by name...That is because they are unable to understand how profound was the impression made by the kindness they showed me, a kindness which produced the little good there is left me in my heart. This finds its source in that first education and in the guidance that these men of God were able to give my spirit and my young heart." These words are a testament to the effectiveness of their methods.

[62] The rule of life the young boys were to follow underwent three drafts, indicating the seriousness with which Eugène took his responsibilities as their director. Further evidence of his dedication to the boys can be found in the arrangements he made to receive papal approval for his boys to receive an indulgence which was granted in 1814 for a period of thirty years. That same year, Pope Pius VII was released after six years in captivity. During his journey back to Rome, the people of France cheered for him in the streets. Father de Mazenod and his sodality were in the crowds cheering the Pontiff as he passed through Aix, and the Holy Father gave the group a special blessing.

follow this rule of life, expulsion from the group was possible.[63] The boys in the group were required to attend Mass every day, go to Confession once per month, and to "live in a manner so as to be able to receive holy Communion frequently." Eugène demanded that those in his charge "keep alive the example which the first Christians had given to the world."

The strict rules did not, as one might think, deter young boys from joining Father de Mazenod's group. The number of members reached twenty-three by the end of 1813, and by the end of 1817 their membership swelled to nearly three hundred, a growth rate that alarmed some people in Aix.[64] According to Eugène, almost all of his boys went on to produce good fruit:

> I trained a good number of them in virtue. I saw some two hundred eighty of them gathered around me, and those who today still remain faithful to the principles that I had the happiness of instilling in their souls and who do honor to their faith in every rank of society or in the sanctuary, will uphold for a long time, either in Aix or in the other

---

[63] By Pielorsz's count there were sixty-four expulsions between 1813 and 1821.

[64] Not all were pleased with Eugène's efforts to form a youth group. In 1817, a pious woman wrote to her friends, "What a wretched liking these children have adopted for this congregation which contradicts their own tastes, passions and the entertainments of their peers. It is because the Abbé in question has the baleful power of making himself loved and feared by that mob of little anti-christs. If one or the other has the misfortune to come into contact with him for a few moments, that is it for him; he is finished. He knows the art of bewitching them…It is true he knows so well how to captivate them…If one of these children falls ill, he will have no one but Abbé de Mazenod who knows the secret formula of seizing even their last breath because he no longer leaves their side; and if that individual dies, he dies in his arms."

places where they are dispersed, the reputation that this congregation had rightly acquired for itself while I was able to care for it.

The sodality met in the morning and afternoon of all Sundays, Thursdays, and feast days for instruction, prayer, Mass, games, and outdoor sports. The chief aim was to develop the young boys into solid Christian men. Pursuant to that end, prayer and Mass were a priority, and the boys received instruction during resting periods of games. However, Eugène did not consider the games an opportunity to give the boys a break from spiritual matters; he viewed them "as direct a means of going to God as prayer is." Heavy emphasis was placed on the boys enjoying the meetings. The rules dictated that the boys "will run, they will jump, they will sing, in a word, they will enjoy themselves as much as they can, intimately convinced that the more they enjoy themselves, the more faithful they are being to this article of the rule and the spirit behind it." Eugène knew that, if his young men hated attending the meetings, they would cease to be members of the sodality.

Eugène sought to guide his youth association in all aspects of life, "that they give themselves to the utmost joy, to the greatest exhilaration with a view to pleasing God, conforming themselves to the precept of the Apostle that whether we eat, or drink, or are doing whatever other thing we do it in the name of Jesus Christ Our Lord." Knowing most of the boys were students, Eugène, therefore, impressed upon them the importance of carrying out their scholastic duties and offering their schoolwork to the Lord. He also counseled them to accept in a penitential spirit any boredom that might occur in their studies.

In his spiritual advisements, Eugène warned the boys that some people might look down upon them for having strong values, but he noted those individuals were "unworthy of bearing the name Christian and to belong to the Immortal One who has triumphed and who has gained the world by virtue of his Cross and humiliation." To survive the taunts of others, Eugène encouraged the boys to pick up the Cross of Christ, advising them to display a crucifix in their rooms. As further protection against the sneers and resistance they would face in the practice of virtue, Eugène taught them to make frequent use of ejaculatory prayers so that the rejection they would face could "never cool or put out the fire of charity which should always be burning in their hearts."

Moreover, Eugène instructed the members of the youth sodality to perform acts of mercy, as well. His rule of life for the young boys put protocols in place for whenever a member fell ill. Infirmarians were appointed and were to care for the ailing members of the society. Prayers and Masses were said for those who were sick. Eugène even had to administer Last Rites to some members. On those instances, Eugène praised the members of his youth sodality for the reverence and respect with which they carried out their duties and for how they came to the aid of their dying companion. Eugène himself was extremely dedicated to all those who were in his care that were on their death bed.[65] In further practice of virtue, the group chose to use some of the money budgeted for snacks at their meetings in the year 1815 to have Masses said for the souls in purgatory. Eugène reported that this money enabled thirty-three Masses to be said with this intention.

---

[65] As previously noted, care for the sick was a practice of Eugène's in Palermo, and one he continued in Aix and throughout the remainder of his life, especially when one of his Oblates was in danger of death. A letter from Fortuné de Mazenod to Eugène's father dated April 1, 1819, testifies to this: "[Y]ou know he does not leave for a moment the souls confided to his care when they are in danger of death."

Prison Ministry

For a brief period prior to entering the seminary, Eugène worked for an organization charged with managing the prisons of Aix-en-Provence, so he knew that prison conditions were deplorable. When he returned to his hometown, Eugène volunteered to serve as a prison chaplain, and his missionary society would continue serving as prison chaplains until the expulsion of all religious orders from France in 1903.

Father Eugène de Mazenod visited prisoners almost every day, teaching them, trying to convert them, hearing confessions, and leading them in hymns and night prayer. He was especially concerned about prisoners condemned to death. Eugène celebrated Mass for the prisoner in his cell just before his execution and would walk with him to the guillotine. This behavior drew the attention of many in Aix, for it was not the prevailing practice of the day to admit condemned criminals to Holy Communion.

One notable criminal to whom Eugène de Mazenod ministered was a woman known by the name La Germaine. Her atrocious crimes had drawn the scorn and ire of the community. She was shunned and condemned to the gallows. In the eyes of all, she was unworthy of life and her inherent dignity. However, Saint Eugène de Mazenod took pity on La Germaine. He decided to treat her like a human being, visiting her in her cell and speaking with her. Because of his kindness and concern for her soul, she converted. Eugène granted her absolution and admitted her to Communion before her execution, knowing of her conversion and the purity of her soul in her final days. Eugène whispered words of consolation to La Germaine as she walked to the gallows. Those who were present for the execution were moved by the charitable actions of Saint Eugène de Mazenod.

The love Eugène had for prisoners extended to the 2,000 Austrian prisoners of war that had been brought to Aix as a result of Napoleon's wars. When a typhus epidemic hit the prison camp and their chaplain died, Eugène volunteered to be their new chaplain. Typhus was still present in the camp, but in conformity with his previous actions, Eugène showed no concern for his health, braving the threat of typhus which he eventually caught.

The Oblates

Cannot Work Alone

Eugène de Mazenod was sick for months, and all assumed he was dying. On March 14, 1814, he received the Anointing of the Sick. However, the Holy Association for Christian Youth held out hope and prayed fervently. The prayers of his youth sodality were answered, and he recovered on May 3, 1814, the day when King Louis XVIII triumphantly returned to Paris, marking the start of the Bourbon Restoration.

This illness made Eugène realize the work he was doing was too important for him to undertake it alone. He felt called to start a missionary society. "I have a feeling that some outside force compelled me to make a decision of the most serious nature," he wrote to a friend from the seminary. The desire to found a missionary society was not an invention of his own mind, but a divine calling.

Pursuant to the Lord's will, Eugène began to recruit priests to join his proposed missionary society. He sent letters to priests not just in his own diocese, but priests from all over Provence. Of all the priests to whom Eugène sent an invitation, one stood out to him as being necessary to the success of the missionary society.

Henri Tempier

Father Henri Tempier, a young priest, received a letter proposing that he join the sender in establishing a missionary society dedicated to serving the most abandoned. As he read this letter and learned specifics of the plan, Tempier felt something stir within his soul. He knew what the sender proposed would be an ambitious project, but one that could do a tremendous amount of good if successful. The more he read of the plan and the more he read the flattering words the sender wrote about him, the more eager he became to accept the proposal. However, when he reached the end of the letter and saw no signature, his heart sank thinking someone was pulling a prank on him. He sadly set the letter aside. When the sender followed up on the letter and remembered to sign his name, Father Henri Tempier realized it was no prank and enthusiastically accepted the offer to join Saint Eugène de Mazenod's apostolate.

Early in their correspondence, Eugène knew that he and Father Tempier were of one mind when it came to the work of evangelization. The former wrote to the latter, "[T]he interior life of our community needs a priest who thinks like you. I am so convinced of it that last night I told the vicar general that I would not commit myself to form this community if you were not a part of it." Fathers de Mazenod and Tempier began eagerly working towards getting Tempier released from his diocese to join de Mazenod's community.

Father Henri Tempier became an instrumental figure in the life of Saint Eugène de Mazenod. From the time he first joined Father Eugène in Aix until the day Bishop de Mazenod died, Tempier was his best friend and right-hand man, and he knew better than anyone how to handle things when Eugène lost his temper. Whenever Eugène erupted into an outburst, Tempier waited for the tantrum to conclude and would simply say, "What then?"

Founding a Missionary Society

Soon, Fathers de Mazenod and Tempier were joined by four others, and it became necessary to organize themselves as a diocesan congregation. Eugène did not desire to start something new, but rather replace those congregations that had vanished amid the upheaval of the French Revolution. In their petition to the vicars general of Aix, dated January 25, 1816 (Feast of the Conversion of Saint Paul), the community stated it was "deeply concerned about the deplorable situation of Provence's small towns and villages which have almost entirely lost the faith." It described the situation as one of "obduracy" and "indifference." Furthermore, the founding members informed the diocese that, if approved, they would spend their lives "in prayer, meditation on the sacred truths, cultivation of the virtues, the study of Sacred Scripture and the Fathers of the Church, the study of dogmatic and moral theology, preaching, and the direction of youth." It was to be a missionary society where one would enter with the intention of remaining there for one's entire life, and after two years in the society, membership would become permanent. Eugène's bishop approved of their plan, and they adopted the name "The Missioners of Provence."

Father Eugène de Mazenod and his companions felt a strong desire to live in community with one another. Arrangements were made to purchase a convent just outside of town, but those plans fell through. Eugène was, however, successful in purchasing a convent in town and the adjoining church. The living quarters were small, and the church was in rough shape. Due to the small amount of space in their new living quarters, Father Eugène de Mazenod slept in the narrow passageway leading to the room where two others slept. The table where they ate their meals was merely a plank which had been set on top of two barrels. The Missioners of Provence dined nightly on a meager meal of rice or semolina soup flavored with almonds and an orange.[66]

The conditions inside the adjoining church were less appealing than their living quarters. According to a letter Eugène

---

[66] Eugène de Mazenod believed oranges were "good for cooling the blood when irritated."

wrote at the time, it rained as much inside the church as it did outside. Against all odds, they were able, with the help of the Holy Association of Christian Youth, to make the necessary repairs in time for Holy Week in 1816.

On Holy Thursday night, while adoring the Blessed Sacrament all night, Eugène de Mazenod and Henri Tempier pledged obedience to one another. They did this without the knowledge of the other members of the Missioners of Provence, for not everyone was willing to fully adopt the vows of religious life at that time.

The Activities of the Society

Establishing a missionary society did not bring an end to Eugène's work with the youth and prisoners. On the contrary, it flourished even more with the help of his missionaries. Eugène's group of missionaries "in a way came forth from [his] heart."[67] Therefore, Eugène integrated the work of ministering to youth and prisoners into his missionary society. When the society eventually expanded, Eugène encouraged every house to have a boys' group attached to it.

However, Eugène saw preaching parish missions as the chief activity of the Congregation. So dedicated was Father de Mazenod to the parish missions that he once walked sixty-six kilometers to a parish mission. He and his companions preached missions in the city of Aix and all throughout Provence. Some of the mission crosses they erected still stand today.

The Missioners of Provence were quite successful in their missions. Eugène is reported to have excelled at reading a parish and adapting to the parish's needs, and he was widely regarded as an excellent preacher. He employed every technique necessary

---

[67] Quote taken from Circular Letter written by Saint Eugène to all Oblates dated February 2, 1857.

to convert the parish.[68] His most beloved characteristic was preaching in a language the people could understand.[69] One of his more dramatic measures was to deliver a sermon on death in front of an open grave while holding a skull. The Missioners of Provence also provided adequate time for parishioners to go to Confession, sitting in the confessional late into the night if necessary. Despite his love for preaching parish missions, Father de Mazenod regarded it as a "perilous ministry," for one could easily get too caught up in oneself, believing that the individual, not the Holy Spirit, was cause of the great work that was being accomplished through preaching.

Soon the Missioners of Provence were in high demand. Many parishes were asking for them to come to their parish, and Eugène and his companions were able to be rather selective with regards to which parishes they chose for their missions. Eugène wrote to the pastor in Barjols in 1818, "More than fifty pastors are asking insistently for a mission… However, I am inclined to give you preference. It seems to me that our duty is to rush to where there is the most urgent need. They asked for us at Marseilles; we could expect consolation there, whereas at Barjols we must await only contradictions and difficulty." Eugène desired to go where the need was greatest, reaching out to the most abandoned, a characteristic he maintained throughout his entire priesthood.

The effect Eugène and his missionaries had on the towns in which they preached extended beyond just religious practice. On February 14, 1820, a veteran of Napoleon's army assassinated the Duc de Berry. In the wake of this crime, anger brewed in

---

[68] In the Rule Eugène de Mazenod composed for the Missionary Oblates of Mary Immaculate, he wrote, "We must spare no effort to extend the Savior's empire and to destroy the dominion of Hell."

[69] "[T]he Gospel must be taught to all and it must be taught in such a way as to be understood," Eugène said in his 1813 Ash Wednesday sermon.

the streets. Fortunately, at that time, the Missioners of Provence were preaching parish missions in an area of France where the anger was on the verge of boiling over and carrying out reprisals against those who opposed the king. Father Eugène de Mazenod, although he abhorred the crime, preached a message of peace from the pulpit, and, following his preaching, he went out into the streets and spoke with the groups forming there. His words had a calming effect on the crowds, and a riot was avoided.

Moreover, a book[70] published in 1980 detailing the history of the Catholic Church in France noted the positive effect the moral theology of Saint Alphonsus Liguori had on the people of France and credited Eugène and his missionary society with its propagation. If Eugène had not encountered Liguori's teachings while in exile, the people of France might not have had the grace of learning that system of moral theology which was of great benefit to them.

Eugène, the Oblates, and Their Mission

Although the founder and superior general for life of the Missioners of Provence, Eugène de Mazenod never viewed himself as the boss. In his mind, God was in charge. Eugène only saw himself as a father to the members of the society. His all-or-nothing approach to any task resulted in his spiritual fatherhood producing emotion akin to that of a loving parent. When one of his priests fell ill, he wrote, "If I showed exteriorly all the anguish I am going through, they would take me for a madman, when in truth I am simply a man who, so I wish to believe, is rendered very imperfect by my love." Eugène felt he had the responsibility to care for the priests of the Missioners of Provence and help them achieve holiness. He once wrote, "I have no servants in the Congregation; I have only well-loved

---

[70] François Lebrun, ed. *Histoire des catholiques en France: Du XVe siecle a nos jours* (history of Catholics in France from the 15th century to our day).

sons who are foremost in my heart, sons whom I mention before God." The Congregation was not his own; he was merely its steward.

This steward tried his best to guide his oblates to follow the example of the Apostles by continuing Christ's work of Salvation. Their outreach to the most abandoned was not merely acts of charity for the sake of doing good deeds. They sought to bring others to Christ through their ministry. Eugène passed his vision onto his oblates when he wrote:

> We are, or we ought to be, holy priests who consider themselves happy and very happy to devote their fortune, their health, their life in the service and for the glory of our God. We are put on earth, particularly those of our house, to sanctify ourselves while helping each other by our example, our words and our prayers. Our Lord Jesus Christ has left to us the task of continuing the great work of the redemption of mankind. It is towards this unique end that all our efforts must tend; as long as we will not have spent our whole life and given all our blood to achieve this, we have nothing to say; especially when as yet we have given only a few drops of sweat and a few spells of fatigue. This spirit of being wholly devoted to the glory of God, the service of the Church, and the salvation of souls is the spirit that is proper to our Congregation, a small one, to be sure, but which will always be powerful as long as she is holy. Our novices must steep themselves in these thoughts, which must sink deep in them and be often meditated. Each society in the Church has a spirit which is its own; which is inspired by God according to the circumstances and needs of the times wherein it pleases God to raise these supporting bodies or rather it would be better to say these elite bodies which precede the main army on the march, which excel it in bravery and which thus obtains the more brilliant victories.

Saint Eugène de Mazenod viewed the Congregation as a continuation of the work Jesus sent the twelve Apostles to accomplish. This belief was so entrenched in his mind that he wrote in the Preface to the Rules for the Congregation that "[t]heir Institutor is Jesus Christ, the Son of God Himself; their first fathers the Apostles. They are called to be the Savior's cooperators, the co-redeemers of the human race." There are many other writings where the founder compared the Oblates' ministry to that of the Apostles.

Expansion

In 1818, the bishop of Digne became impressed with the work the Missioners of Provence were doing and invited them to establish a second house in his diocese in the hope of restoring the Marian shrine, Notre Dame du Laus. They would care for the large number of pilgrims visiting the shrine in the summer and would have time for missions in the winter. Eugène, an ever-devoted son of Mary, was eager to accept. For two and a half months, he worked diligently to take care of all of the necessary details for this next step of his tiny society. The decision necessitated establishing a rule of life applicable to all Oblate houses, the convocation of a general chapter, electing a superior general and other administrators, and taking religious vows.

Eugène spent twelve days at his family's "heap of stones" in Saint Laurent composing the Congregation's first Rule, and a general chapter was convened in October of 1818. Eugène de Mazenod was elected as superior general for life with Father Henri Tempier as second-in-command. The Rule Eugène wrote was the biggest source of controversy at the general chapter. The first part, which detailed the way of life that each house was to follow, was readily accepted. The second part, detailing the religious vows that would be taken by every member of the society, was the specific source of the controversy. The initial vote on the Rule rejected the vows by a vote of four to three. After the vote, Father de Mazenod reminded them that the future of the society rested with the students within their community. It was, therefore, decided that they had a right to vote on the Rule of life they were to follow. The three students who were studying with them at that time were brought in for a second vote. All three students voted in favor of religious vows, and the entirety of the Rule was officially approved. Two of those who had been opposed immediately decided to take their vows. Another asked to take temporary vows, and the final objector asked for a delay.

Controversy

Not everyone in France was pleased with the work Father de Mazenod was doing. Some of the priests of Aix did not like how Eugène was not assigned to a parish and was drawing people away from their parishes to attend services at his Church of the Mission. Eugène also caused a stir when he decided that the boys of his sodality would receive First Holy Communion and Confirmation as a group, separate from the youth of their home parishes. The animosity towards Eugène and his oblates would continue to grow both within and outside of his diocese as the Missioners of Provence group did. Soon, action would become necessary to protect their society from dissolution.

Marseilles

Fortuné de Mazenod and Marseilles

Despite their best efforts at survival, the Missioners of Provence felt that the future of their organization was in peril. Pressure mounted from outside their community, endangering their future. Bishops turned on them despite the wonderful things they had done in their dioceses. Eugène de Mazenod knew action needed to be taken.

Word began to spread that relations between the Church and the government were improving and that the government was going to allow the Church to re-establish the Diocese of Marseilles.[71] This gave Eugène an idea as to how he could preserve his group of missionaries. If they had a bishop as a supporter, this would give legitimacy and protection to the Missioners of Provence. Eugène decided to campaign to have his uncle, Fortuné de Mazenod, named as the bishop for the newly revived Diocese of Marseilles. The plan was bold, but Eugène knew he needed to try.

Eugène faced an uphill battle in convincing the Minister of Public Worship to nominate Fortuné de Mazenod as bishop of Marseilles, but he began making the necessary overtures anyway. After months of work, it looked like he was going to be successful, but at the last minute, his plan hit a snag. The Minister of

---

[71] During the French Revolution, the number of dioceses in France was reduced in order to reduce the power of the Church in France.

Public Worship offered the job to the nephew as opposed to the uncle. Declining the offer, Eugène renewed his request that his uncle be named bishop of Marseilles, a request that was eventually granted.

Although Eugène's plan succeeded in France, it would still need to be successful in Italy as well. Fortuné de Mazenod was still living in Italy and needed to be convinced to return to a land where he was almost murdered in the streets during the French Revolution. Luckily, Eugène managed to convince Fortuné de Mazenod to agree to become a bishop, but only on the condition that Eugène and Father Henri Tempier would serve as his vicars general. This was all done before the appointment became official, however. Soon word spread that Fortuné was to be the new bishop of Marseilles, and the elder Father de Mazenod, along with his two brothers, arrived in Marseilles in December of 1817 to a large crowd.

Just when the appointment was about to be finalized, the Church's relationship with the government soured yet again, and the restoration of the See of Marseilles was put on hold. Fortuné, with nowhere else to go, went to Aix to live with Eugène's Congregation and spent several years waiting for the situation to be resolved.

The Fate of Eugène's Father

According to Eugène, Charles-Antoine de Mazenod had a "stormy" youth. Despite love affairs and living beyond his means, Eugène's father always remained faithful to the Blessed Virgin Mary. This practice may have temporarily ceased when Charles-Antoine left the Faith for a period of time while in exile. By 1815, however, he had returned to practicing Catholicism and attributed his survival of an 1816 illness to the Blessed Virgin Mary's intercession. From that point forward, he accepted all his hardships as reparation for his sins. Charles-Antoine spent the final two years of his life translating an Italian biography of Saint Alphonse Liguori into French.

When the brothers de Mazenod returned to France, Charles-Antoine Mazenod remained in Marseilles with Le Chevalier when Fortuné went to live in Aix. Fortuné journeyed to Marseilles to visit his brother once per month, but the rest of the family rarely visited him. When Charles-Antoine eventually became fatally ill, Marie-Rose refused to pay his medical bills. This forced Fortuné to borrow five hundred francs for his brother's care. When Charles-Antoine passed away on October 10, 1820, at the age of seventy-five, he died virtually penniless, and, again, Marie-Rose refused to give money to the de Mazenod men for the funeral expenses. Fortuné was forced to borrow more money. At the moment of his death on October 10, 1820, two priests were by his side: his brother, Fortuné, and his son, Saint Eugène de Mazenod.

Bishop and Vicar General de Mazenod

When the See of Marseilles was officially restored in August of 1823, Fortuné's appointment as bishop became official. Pursuant to the agreement made prior to Fortuné agreeing to become a bishop, Eugène and Henri Tempier moved to Marseilles to serve as his vicars general. The new bishop's nephew saw this as a way to further strengthen the Congregation's stability and was willing to accept the move. However, Tempier needed to be persuaded because he felt he did not have the courage needed to do the job well. After Eugène convinced Tempier to accept the position of vicar general, they left Aix for Marseilles, thinking they had taken a positive step for the missionary society.

Fortuné quickly won over the hearts of the people of Marseilles. This was not the case for Eugène. He was suspected of running the diocese solely for his Congregation's benefit. "I was welcomed like a stranger and an intruder," he would later write. Yet, Eugène faced the challenges of assisting his uncle in reviving the Diocese of Marseilles with characteristic determination:

This will be, I hope, again to do my duty there, to try by my every zealous effort to bring a little bit of life back into a dead diocese whatever appearance of health it may have; there will no doubt be new crises, there was never a reform without hurting, wounding plenty of people!...But one must have much virtue to sacrifice one's peace for one's duty, to face the hatred and persecution of men precisely so as to do good for men.

Sacrilege in Marseilles

In 1829, while Eugène was vicar general of Marseilles, the Blessed Sacrament was stolen from the Church of Saint Theodore in Marseilles. Later, some workman discovered the Sacred Hosts in a field outside Marseilles. Upon hearing the news, Eugène rushed to the place where they were found, and, with tears running down his cheeks, knelt down to pick up the Eucharistic species. He held them against his heart until a procession could be arranged to take them back to the church.

From that day on, the diocese held an annual octave of atonement around the anniversary of the sacrilege. The Act of Reparation that spontaneously sprang from Eugène's heart on that day was publicly re-read during that octave. On the tenth of these annual ceremonies, Eugène wrote:

> I admit that it gave me an unspeakable consolation to think that I have been responsible for procuring for Our Lord the glory given him at Saint Theodore's for the last ten years. Today again I offered him very simply and without any mixture of vainglory, all the love and reparation shown Him and I offered it to Him with joy as though it were all from me in atonement of my own irreverence and my insufficient correspondence with the great lights and inspirations God has been pleased to communicate to me for many years, in the adorable Sacrament of the Altar.

The incident involving the sacrilege that occurred in Marseilles is just one anecdote from the life of Saint Eugène de Mazenod that displays his respect and love for the Blessed Sacrament. His contemporaries reported that, on numerous occasions, Eugène burst into tears in front of the Eucharist. He once mused, "During my Adoration of the Blessed Sacrament exposed, I was held by the thought that it was impossible to be better off. Is it not a foretaste of Heaven to find oneself in the presence of Jesus, prostrate at His feet to adore Him, to love Him and, to await from His bounty the graces we need?" To Eugène, nothing was more precious in this world than the Eucharist.

Crisis in the Congregation

The decision by Eugène and Tempier to move to Marseilles to be Bishop Fortuné de Mazenod's vicars general did not sit well with the rest of the Congregation. Two of them wrote to the bishop in their home diocese and asked that their vows be declared null. In October of 1823, the bishop agreed, and the priests left the Congregation. A third priest was also released from his vows by his bishop and left the Congregation as well. Eugène was hurt by the move and wondered why the bishops, who knew about the vows, found no problem with them until the priests became dissatisfied with Eugène's actions.

Furthermore, Eugène was saddened and confused when he heard some bishops had made harsh and hurtful comments about him and his organization. For eight years Eugène and his missionaries had served their dioceses, providing parish missions that improved the spiritual lives of their flocks. Now he was facing fierce opposition from the very people he had tried to help.

The departures put the Congregation in serious jeopardy. With so few members, losing even just one member was an ordeal. Moreover, if a bishop could declare their vows null, more bishops might recall other priests that had joined the

Congregation. Eugène wrote numerous letters defending his Congregation, but little success came from these appeals. One bishop finally agreed to not force any priest to leave the Congregation who did not want to leave, and the archbishop of Aix apologized for his behavior and the hurtful words he had spoken about Eugène.

In October of 1824, Eugène returned to Aix for a general chapter and brutally flogged himself in front of the remaining members, to show them he was sorry for not consulting them about the move to Marseilles. After the flogging, he asked if he should resign as superior general. They immediately placed their trust in him once more, averting further danger from within the Congregation.

The danger from outside the Congregation remained, however, for at any time a bishop could have destroyed Missioners of Provence by removing his priests from the Congregation. The appointment of Fortuné de Mazenod as bishop of Marseilles did not have the protective effect Eugène intended it to have when he plotted to have his uncle elevated to the episcopacy. Further action was needed.

Papal Approbation

The Need

The Missioners of Provence were under threat. Several bishops across France were against them. At any point, a bishop could have destroyed their organization with one simple move. The future looked bleak. It seemed only papal approval could preserve them. However, if the Pope did not approve their organization, it would surely be their death knell.

Eugène wavered for a long time on whether or not to go to Rome. It may seem baffling that someone who was as passionate and stubborn as Saint Eugène de Mazenod would hesitate to go to Rome to seek papal approbation. As Bishop Jeancard described the situation, "He who did not know how to retreat when faced with obstacles which appeared insurmountable, which reared up in his path, did not find entirely in himself the courage he needed to go to seek the approval of the Congregation." Yet, it must be recalled that to act was against Eugène's inclinations. By nature, he only took action if he thought it necessary. Another explanation for his hesitance might lie in his firm belief that, if something is not successful, it must not be the Lord's will.[72] If Eugène went to Rome and did not receive

---

[72] Eugène once said, "My policy is to lend myself to all inspirations. If God wills them, nothing will be able to prevent them. And if God does not will them, they shall fail of their own accord without any interference from me."

approval from the Holy Father, it would surely mean his religious community was not the will of God.

Eugène would not take decisive action until one of the more quiet members of the Congregation, Father Albini, pushed the superior general with both hands and pleaded with him, "Go, Father, go!" That gesture made the course of action clear: Saint Eugène de Mazenod would go to Rome.

The Papal Audience

On October 30, 1825, Eugène began his journey to Rome to seek papal approbation for the group now calling themselves the Oblates of Saint Charles.[73] His first step was to seek the personal assistance of cardinals with whom he was acquainted to help him gain an audience with the Pope. Cardinal de Gregorio, a former Black Cardinal, pledged his help, and Eugène began to wait for word on when his audience would be.

Weeks went by, and Eugène lost his patience. On December 20, 1825, he went to the papal residence and demanded an audience with the Pope. The staff member to whom he spoke was so low in rank that he could not get Eugène in to see the Pope that day, as it was the last day for audiences before Christmas. However, just as the staff member was leaving to resume his duties, Monsignor Barberini, who had promised Eugène a papal audience, arrived at the Vatican. Father de Mazenod chided him for not following through on his promise to arrange a papal audience, and the monsignor, recognizing the scolding was deserved, took him up to the waiting room of the Pope's office.

Eugène patiently waited his turn and was finally able to speak with Pope Leo XII for forty-five minutes. He told of all the good his Congregation was doing and asked for a papal approbation. The Holy Father was especially pleased to hear how

---

[73] Saint Charles was the patron saint of the de Mazenod family.

one of the youngest oblates had converted a great number of Protestants. Despite being greatly impressed by the small Congregation, the Pope said that, with the large number of requests received for such approbations, the Vatican had established a precedent of granting a message of support, without formal approbation. Father de Mazenod boldly stated that such a decision would not satisfy him. In response, the Pope told him to go to the pro-secretary of the Congregation of Bishops and Religious, the arch-priest Pietro Adinolfi, and give him all the necessary documents for him to make a report. The Pontiff told Eugène to instruct Adinolfi to have the report to him by Friday of that week. Lastly, Eugène asked the Pope if it was best to continue under the name Oblates of Saint Charles or if they should change their name again to "Oblates of Mary Immaculate." The Pope tabled the issue, telling Eugène to worry about that later.

Approval

After the papal audience concluded, Eugène went to a church to pray a prayer of thanksgiving and then went directly to Adinolfi who spoke politely with Eugène for a while and, like the Pope, was impressed by Eugène's Congregation, but reminded him that papal approbations had become rare. Before leaving, he instructed Eugène to return Saturday morning so they could discuss what the Pope had said during their meeting on Friday. As he left, Eugène told Adinolfi, "I leave this matter in your hands. I ask only God's designs be fulfilled."

That Saturday, Eugène went to Adinolfi's residence to hear the news. The pro-secretary had indeed recommended the message of support without formal approbation, but Pope Leo XII told him, "No, this society pleases me; I know the good that it is doing." Eugène wept with joy and ran to a church to offer a prayer of thanksgiving.

Final Steps

Nothing was official yet, but the Pope had made his wishes clear. Next, a team of cardinals would go over the Rule of the society and would make changes where necessary. Normally, Eugène possessed little patience, but knowing approbation was almost guaranteed, he was more than willing to wait the months it took to finalize the approbation.

While the deliberations were taking place, three bishops from France sent a letter to the Vatican urging them not to approve Eugène de Mazenod's oblates. In this letter, these bishops indirectly showed their Gallican beliefs by questioning the Pope's authority to make such a decision. The letter backfired, strengthening the case for approving the Oblates.

The cardinals tasked with reviewing the report approved it on February 15 with only a few minor changes to the Rule. Eugène took the changes and worked long into the night in order to put the finishing touches on the Rule. Everything was finished on the 16th, and the official approbation from the Pope came on February 17, 1826.

Next, the two hundred pages of the hand-written rule needed to be recopied so that they included the cardinals' changes. Eugène worked day and night on this project and finished the job in three days, inflicting writer's cramp on himself in the process. After more clerical work had been done, public promulgation of the approbation finally arrived on March 21, 1826.

Oblates of Mary Immaculate

Despite Saint Charles being his patron saint, the name Oblates of Saint Charles never felt right to Charles Joseph Eugène de Mazenod. The Supreme Pontiff had given him no definitive answer on the matter of a name change during his papal audience. When Eugène received the documents officially approving his Congregation, he was delighted to see the Pope had referred to them as the "Missionary Oblates of

Mary Immaculate, conceived without sin." Eugène wrote to Father Tempier in response to this particular part of the approbation: "[I]t is the Church who has given us that beautiful name; we receive it with respect, love, and gratitude, proud of our dignity and of the rights it gives us to the protection of her who is all-powerful in God's presence. Let us delay no longer in taking upon ourselves that beautiful name whenever prudence permits." In other letters back to France, Eugène expressed great joy over the name: "This name pleases the heart and the ear." He also added that the name was "a passport to Heaven."

Overworked

During his entire life, Eugène de Mazenod was a tireless worker, rarely allowing himself a chance to rest. He was up until 11:00 P.M. most nights and would wake up at 4:00 A.M. The notes Eugène took on retreats early in his priesthood are filled with self-chastisements for focusing too much on work and neglecting his own physical and spiritual health. Sometimes he expressed a desire to retire to a quiet monastery to live a cloistered lifestyle, always returning to his work knowing that he was called to public ministry.

The papal approbation inspired Eugène to work increasingly harder in order not to disappoint the Pope. Eugène, already an extremely hard worker, pushed himself too far when he increased his workload. In May of 1829, the forty-six-year-old priest collapsed from total exhaustion.

Soon, he was up on his feet and back to his zealous work. This worried Father Henri Tempier who knew Eugène had not given himself enough of a rest. Tempier's patience gave out, and he ordered Eugène to go on a sabbatical to Switzerland. Eugène, who had pledged obedience to Tempier on Holy Thursday in 1816, obeyed and went to Switzerland to rest for several months.

Abandoned

Elevation to the Episcopacy

While Eugène was resting in Switzerland, word came of the July Revolution of 1830. The Bourbon Monarchy was once again overthrown and replaced by the Duke of Orleans. The relationship between the Church and the government worsened during what was known as the July Monarchy. It was improved relations between the government and the Church that allowed for the restoration of the See of Marseilles, but the newly established government put its future in jeopardy.

Bishop Fortuné de Mazenod began to hear rumors that, upon his death or retirement, the government would once again prevent the Church from having a diocese in Marseilles. Not wanting his people to be without a bishop, the elderly bishop began scheming to protect the future of his diocese. His plan centered around his vicar general and nephew. If Eugène was named as a bishop *in partibus infidelium* (a bishop with no diocese to oversee), there would be a logical successor in place in the event of his death, preventing an attempt by the government to shut down the diocese.

The Church agreed to name Eugène titular bishop of Icosia. Eugène abhorred the idea of running a diocese, but consented to becoming a bishop on the condition he was not given a diocese. He did not mind the title because of the boon it would be for his Congregation, and he liked the idea of being able to ordain his oblates.

The consecration of Bishop Eugène de Mazenod had to be carried out in secret. According to the Concordat of 1801, the agreement between Napoleon Bonaparte and Pope Pius VII, the government of France had the right to nominate bishops for the Church's approval. Despite the fact Napoleon was no longer in power, the agreement was still in effect. While the elderly bishop's nephew was not technically being appointed as a bishop of a diocese in France, he would nevertheless be a bishop in France. The Church felt that there would be no violation of the concordat by consecrating Eugène de Mazenod a bishop for a diocese in Africa that no longer existed, but sensitive to how it would look to the French government, the Church was careful to avoid any word of the elevation of this priest to the episcopacy for fear of further straining relations with the French government. On October 14, 1832, Eugène de Mazenod was consecrated a bishop in the Church of Saint Sylvester where his childhood tutor, Don Bartolo Zinelli, had been buried.

The Trials of the Bishop of Icosia

When the government found out about the new Bishop de Mazenod, suspicion arose, and they began surveillance of Eugène as he went about his normal duties as vicar general of Marseilles and superior general of the Missionary Oblates of Mary Immaculate. Suddenly, word came that Eugène was needed immediately at the Vatican. Ever obedient to the Chair of Peter, Eugène left as soon as possible. In Rome, he learned of charges the French government was making against him. During a lengthy meeting with Pope Gregory XVI, Eugène defended himself. The Pope saw the truth of the matter and allowed him to return to Marseilles.

Not long after he returned to Marseilles, the government revoked his citizenship and the rights awarded to citizens. On the advice of two prominent lawyers, Eugène sued the government, but he soon received word that the Pope would prefer it if he did not further agitate the government. Bishop Eugène de Mazenod sadly, but obediently, dropped the lawsuit. He was forced to resign as vicar general, leave Marseilles, and live with his oblates at Notre Dame du Laus.

However, Eugène would not be absent from Marseilles permanently. When a cholera epidemic hit the city of Marseilles in 1835, Eugène defied the government and returned to his city to minister to the sick. In this time of crisis, the government looked the other way and allowed him to care for the people.

Ultramontanism

The obedience he showed to the Pope by dropping the lawsuit is characteristic of his life-long obedience to the Pope. He once wrote:

> There are two types of opinion: political, on the one hand, and religious on the other. Each person is free to think as he likes on the former; one may even hold one's silence, when one's thoughts differ from the ordinary, and that is what I do. But it is quite different with the second type. Once you are a Catholic, you are not allowed to pick and choose. One must of necessity adopt the decisions of the one established to teach; and if there is schism, it is the party who is not with Peter who has gone astray. Such is my invariable manner of thought; I would not swerve from it, even were some decision handed down by [the Magisterium] that goes against my own views.

The respect and honor Eugène gave to the Pope dated back to his early years. While in Naples, Eugène overheard his father and a group of adults discuss an impending invasion of the Papal States by the French army. One priest criticized Pope Pius VI for ordering prayers instead of deploying an army. Eugène knew he should have kept his mouth shut, but when no one spoke up to defend the Pope, the young Frenchman could no longer hold his tongue. Without regard for how others might view him, Eugène broke his silence and came to the defense of the Holy Father.

Saint Eugène also believed that one should pray for the Pope every day. While in the seminary, he wrote to his mother, "We must not let a day go by, or ever say our prayers, without beseeching the Supreme Pontiff to watch over his Church, and to strengthen more and more his earthly representative, and uphold him in the painful circumstances he is in."

Similarly, Eugène had a great love for the Church as a whole. In a book he owned, a young Eugène de Mazenod wrote this as a clarification to anyone who might be confused upon discovering he owned it:

> I firmly believe everything the Church commands me to believe, and I abhor Jansenist and other errors which are contained in this book. This is written to make it known that even though I own this book, I give no adherence whatever to tenets contrary to the constant teaching of the holy, Catholic, apostolic, Roman Church which is one and indivisible and will remain so to the end of the world.

Saint Eugène knew that the Church was founded by Jesus Christ. Therefore, the Church and its earthly leader deserved his unwavering loyalty. Eugène always strove to carry out his priestly duties in line with this in mind. That is why, despite his assurance from two prominent lawyers that his lawsuit would be successful, Eugène dropped his civil case against the government.

Citizenship Restored

Eugène's trials eventually came to an end later in 1835 through the intervention of the Queen, whom he had met while in exile, and two of his oblates, Tempier and Joseph Hippolyte Guibert. However, Eugène was reluctant to accept the terms that had been agreed upon by the government and his intercessors. He did not want to sign an oath of loyalty. Bishop de Mazenod was loyal to God and the Pope, but he could not see himself professing loyalty to a government or a king. The ever-patient Tempier lost his temper while trying to talk Eugène into accepting the deal. "[I]f...you wish to get out of the state which I might call miserable, it will be necessary for you to give in a little and to yield to the way your friends feel; they have done nothing which would be unworthy of you and for nothing in the world would they wish to advise you take a debasing and improper step." The influence of his uncle and the two oblates ultimately wore down Eugène, and he agreed to the deal, crediting his friends' persistence for his about-face.

Bishop of Marseilles

Bishop of Marseilles

Just when his friends and uncle thought Eugène had come to his senses, he once again shocked them by refusing to become the bishop of his uncle's diocese. His uncle wanted to retire, but Eugène had no desire of taking over for him. After being forced into exile for the second time in his life, his friends had thought he would gladly accept the responsibility that was being offered to him. Despite already being a titular bishop of a defunct diocese and being a vicar general of the diocese he was being asked to take over, Eugène still resisted the efforts to make him the new bishop. Like his uncle before him, Eugène needed to be talked into becoming the bishop of Marseilles.

Fathers Henri Tempier and Jacques Jeancard, priest of the Diocese of Marseilles and later bishop of Ceramis, led the campaign to get him to accept the bishopric. "I am speaking to you as a friend and confidant of your most secret thoughts; you would be wrong to refuse a diocese if they wished to put you in charge of one," Tempier wrote to him.

Eugène eventually came around to Tempier's way of thinking and agreed to become the bishop of Marseilles, claiming to do so only because of the influence of his friends. "Rest assured that you and my friends had a great deal to do with this resolve because it is not right for you to be saddened in your affection for me and the desires which it inspires in you," Saint Eugène de Mazenod wrote to his best friend.

Acquiescing to his friends' desires did not remove the trepidation Eugène felt towards accepting responsibility for a diocese. He felt unworthy. While on retreat prior to taking up his position, Eugène stated that he could only carry out the duties of a bishop with the help of the Holy Spirit:

> It is the Holy Spirit abiding in me that must henceforth rule, as complete master, all my thoughts, desires, and affections and my entire will. I must be attentive to all His inspirations, listening to them in the silence of prayer, following them and obeying them in such outward actions as they indicate. I must avoid, with general care, whatever may tend to grieve that Divine Spirit, or to weaken His power or action in my soul. I must purify myself by a daily repentance of my faults, which I will renounce with sighs of deepest compunction.

On October 2, 1837, almost thirty-five years after he had returned from exile via that very same port city, Eugène de Mazenod was officially installed as bishop of Marseilles.

The Black Beast

As bishop, Eugène de Mazenod was, like he had been for most of his priesthood, a polarizing figure. One of the first challenges he faced as bishop was winning over the priests of his diocese. Charles-Antoine once stated that when giving orders, Eugène could be "almost as despotic as Monsieur Bonaparte." That may have been due to Eugène's natural impatience.

Some of the priests of his diocese, annoyed by the great number of reforms their new bishop wanted to implement, gave him the nickname "bête noire" or "black beast." Eugène wanted to improve the formation of the clergy to meet the needs of the rapidly expanding city. He worked hard at teaching them how to preach more effectively and placed his oblates in charge of training new priests for the diocese. Furthermore, he wished to institute houses where priests could live in community, thereby ending the practice of priests living on their own or with their parents and siblings.

Loved by His Flock

The people of Marseilles, on the other hand, had great love and respect for their new bishop. Despite being a high-ranking member of the clergy, Eugène continued to reach out to those he considered abandoned. He did not allow his administrative duties to prevent him from serving others. "I am not a bishop to write books," he once said.

The youth of Marseilles were especially fond of their bishop. Eugène's work with the youth, which he started in the early days of his priesthood, continued as bishop. He would often go with groups of boys on trips to fish or to hike in the mountains.

Many in his diocese marveled at how this great prelate would often go to the homes of the poor and the sick to visit them and pray with them. "I confess that, personally, this ministry, so truly pastoral, fills my soul with holy joy," he wrote of these visits. A diocesan priest of Marseilles once reported seeing Bishop Eugène de Mazenod, who was walking down a street in midwinter, stop in the middle of the snowy street, remove his shoes, and give them away to a poor person who had none, an act reminiscent of his declaration that he would be president of the charcoal haulers. He then walked without shoes to a store where he could buy another pair of shoes.

Eugène, desiring to be available to his flock, allowed anyone who wanted to visit him and talk with him the opportunity to do so. His door was open daily from 10:00 A.M. until 2:00 P.M. These offices hours were not just for the wealthy or the important; anyone who wanted to visit and to talk with the bishop could do so. The lines were so long that people brought their lunches to avoid losing their place in line. "The daily audiences take up all my time, yet they are necessary," Eugène wrote of this practice. "It is the duty of a bishop to be accessible to each one of his flock."

These meetings were not the most formal occasions, but Bishop Eugène de Mazenod did expect some level of decorum. One day, a traveler to Marseilles came to visit the bishop. Eugène de Mazenod greeted him, and the man plopped down on an armchair. "Sir, if you really want to sit down, why not take a chair?" Eugène said upon witnessing this. The man quickly took the hint.

In these meetings, Eugène often gave financial aid to those who sought his help which attracted con artists in addition to those in genuine need of the bishop's attention. A well-dressed young man once visited the bishop and began chatting with him. After making small talk for a while, Bishop de Mazenod pressed him for the reason for his visit. The embarrassed young man told him that he was the nephew of another bishop whom he wished to visit, but did not have the necessary funds to make the trip. Bishop de Mazenod responded that the young man's uncle was, in fact, in the building and that he could see him immediately. The young man made a hasty exit.

The Fishwives

Of all the various demographics of people in Marseilles, there was no group more loyal to Bishop Eugène de Mazenod than the fishwives. Eugène took great pleasure in visiting La Criée, the morning fish market, and chatting in Provençal with the fishermen's wives who were tasked with selling the night's catch, matching their wit and colorful language.

One of the fishwives, known as Babeau, had earned the reputation of being the queen of the fishwives. She was a tough woman, once reported as having said, "To bring a woman to her senses is nothing for me, but to flatten a man with my fists and keep at him even when he's down in the gutter until he can't take any more, well, that's my meat." She ruled the fish market, controlling all that occurred there. Despite her gruff personality,

Babeau had been converted by a sermon on the prodigal son which inspired her to marry her common-law husband and, with the encouragement of Saint Eugène de Mazenod, form a sodality of the fishwives.

Babeau's group chose Saint Anne as their patron and were dedicated to caring for the sick and the dying. It was with their aid that Eugène was able to make his way to the homes of those whom he desired to visit. In addition to arranging his visits, the fishwives were ready to defend Eugène if the need arose. When the government ordered the expulsion of all Jesuits, the fishwives posted guards outside the bishop's residence in case the government came to forcibly remove the Jesuits that were living there. In the wake the 1848 elections, there was concern over the safety of Bishop de Mazenod, and the fishwives once again volunteered to protect him.

Calumny

There was a valet working in the bishop's house in Marseilles who was fired in 1838 for dishonesty and flirting with a chambermaid. While Bishop de Mazenod was on a visit to bless a church that had been desecrated, this former valet went to the carriage carrying Eugène and begged for his job back. When the bishop refused, the valet vowed revenge.

While the ceremony was taking place, the valet entered the church and loudly accused Eugène of homosexuality. The people became indignant that someone would accuse their bishop of such behavior, dragged the man out of the church, and threw him in jail. Eugène de Mazenod, however, calmly finished the ceremony. The following day, he wrote, "Evidently God's grace was with me at that moment. I felt neither any hatred nor any desire for vengeance, however justified it might have been. I sincerely felt I should pray for the wicked man…I myself was amazed by my absolute calm. God, grant that I remain inwardly resigned to this new kind of humiliation."

The calumniator spent the remainder of his days serving a five-year prison sentence, dying at the age of thirty-eight. He lived out his days in a state of agony, yelling out blasphemies, despite several exorcisms. Yet, just before he died, he penned a letter to Bishop de Mazenod apologizing and asking for forgiveness.

Simplicity

As bishop, Eugène continued the practice of eating very little supper which he had begun in the early days of his missionary society. Only when he played host to important guests would he relax his policy. However, during Lent he would not eat supper at all. Instead, he remained at his desk working.

Eugène would occasionally serve a more elegant meal when special guests visited the bishop's house. When one of his missionaries returned to France to be consecrated a bishop, Eugène wanted to reward him for his hardships in Canada and served a stuffed pike. He commented that it was probably rare to eat such a fine fish in the missionary field. The priest hesitated and then replied, "Well, no, not really, Monseigneur. You see, we must fish a great deal through the ice to provision the missions for the winter, so the pike are frozen and stored to feed the sled dogs. We eat only the whitefish, trout, and char."

The Accomplishments of Bishop Eugène de Mazenod

An Active Bishop

The passionate personality of Eugène de Mazenod came in handy during the almost twenty-four years he spent as bishop of Marseilles. As previously noted, Eugène de Mazenod wanted to be a part of the lives of the people in his diocese and, therefore, spent a large amount of time visiting the poor and the sick, taking trips with the youth, and holding office hours. This desire spread into their spiritual lives as well. Eugène consecrated new churches,[74] preached, performed Confirmations and other Sacraments, and established January 6 as an annual day of Adoration for his diocese.

Perhaps the greatest impact Bishop Eugène de Mazenod had on his diocese was the large number of groups and institutions he founded to minister to the people of his diocese. Alfred A. Hubenig, O.M.I., in his book *Saint Eugène de Mazenod: Living in the Spirit's Fire*, lists sixteen organizations that Eugène de Mazenod founded or to which he gave his blessing as bishop between the years of 1835 and 1847. Bishop de Mazenod had a philosophy of letting anyone who wanted to start an apostolate to do so. In his mind, if God willed it, it would succeed; if He did not, it would not succeed. One of these groups grew so large

---

[74] During Eugène's time serving the Diocese of Marseilles (both as vicar general and bishop), thirty-eight new parishes were added.

and successful that the priest running it, Father Timon-David, decided to hand it over to a religious order. Bishop de Mazenod would not allow him to do that. Instead, he encouraged him to found his own religious order.

The Sacred Heart

Saint Eugène de Mazenod had long been devoted to the Sacred Heart of Jesus when he became bishop of Marseilles. The rule of life he wrote while he was a student of Don Bartolo Zinelli mentioned devotions to the Sacred Heart. Furthermore, his friendship with Father Magy not only guided Eugène to the priesthood but also added fervor to his devotion to the Sacred Heart. Eugène became so enthusiastic about the Sacred Heart that he suggested to Father Magy the idea of starting an association to help spread this devotion. Eugène also went to the archbishop of Aix during the early years of his priesthood and successfully campaigned for the establishment of a First Friday Exposition of the Blessed Sacrament in the churches of Aix in dedication to the Sacred Heart.

This devotion to the Sacred Heart of Jesus and/or his appointment as bishop of Marseilles appears to be the result of Divine Providence, for the Diocese of Marseilles was the first diocese in the world to be consecrated to the Sacred Heart. To honor this historic event for his diocese, Bishop Eugène de Mazenod established an annual procession on the anniversary of the consecration. One year, it rained heavily all day and night. Although it was looking like the procession would have to be cancelled, the rains ceased just long enough for the procession to take place. Saint Eugène considered this event a miracle.

Building Projects

While Eugène preferred simplicity in his dress, diet, and overall lifestyle, he desired to offer the best to the Lord in religious ceremonies, consistent with his profound love for the liturgy as a young child. Bishop de Mazenod was fond of processions and other ceremonies that made grand offerings to the Creator. This desire also manifested itself in a longing to build beautiful facilities to hold public worship. The Diocese of Marseilles has Saint Eugène de Mazenod to thank for two magnificent churches that still stand in Marseilles, the Cathedral of Saint Mary Major and Notre-Dame de la Garde.

Early in his episcopacy, Saint Eugène de Mazenod began to discuss the need for a new Cathedral. The old Cathedral, La Major, was rundown and had been damaged during the Revolution. In 1837, the same year he was installed as bishop, Eugène requested three million francs from the government to help build a grand Cathedral for the great city of Marseilles. When the government replied that that amount was too much, Eugène reminded them that the custom fees collected by the city of Marseilles was thirty-two million francs. It took years of campaigning and planning, but the project eventually began to appear feasible in 1850 when Eugène and the Minister of Public Worship agreed to a plan to build a new Cathedral in the Romanesque-Byzantine style on the site of the old Cathedral at a cost of five million francs.

The financial costs were large, and Eugène spent most of his episcopacy lobbying for funds to build his Cathedral. The city of Marseilles pledged one million francs in 1846, and in 1852, Louis-Napoleon Bonaparte[75] laid the cornerstone and announced a government subsidy of two and a half million francs. In a report to the Senate in 1858, Bishop Eugène de Mazenod reported that six and a half million francs had been pledged by the city and the state. By 1869, eight years after the death of Saint Eugène de Mazenod, the cost of the project reached ten million francs.

---

[75] Nephew of Napoleon Bonaparte and president of France from 1848–1852 who declared himself Emperor Napoleon III in 1852 on the forty-eighth anniversary of his uncle's coronation.

The Cathedral would not open for public worship until 1893. Bishop Eugène de Mazenod had stated in 1855 that it was his intention to consecrate the new Cathedral to the Sacred Heart of Jesus, but when Pope Leo XIII elevated the Cathedral to a basilica in 1896, it was given the name Saint Mary Major. The church was finally consecrated on May 6, 1897, and the remains of Saint Eugène de Mazenod and the other previous bishops of Marseilles were transferred to the new Cathedral's crypt the following day.

The second building project Eugène undertook while bishop of Marseilles was the construction of the Basilica of Notre-Dame de La Garde, a Neo-Byzantine church on a hill one hundred and sixty meters high, located near the old fort of Marseilles. An oratory was built on the site in the thirteenth century, and in the sixteenth century, a fort was built around it to protect Marseilles from invading forces.

When Fortuné de Mazenod became bishop of Marseilles, he, Eugène, and the oblates began making improvements on the church building including a bell weighing 8,234 kilograms. In 1850, one of the oblates, Father Jean-Antoine Bernard, proposed to Bishop Eugène de Mazenod the idea of building an entirely new church on the site which would have the largest dimensions possible and would be dedicated to Our Lady of the Guard.

Eugène approved of the priest's idea and began to raise funds and to convince the government to cede the land necessary for the project. To secure the funds for the project, Eugène issued a special appeal to the people of Marseilles asking for their generosity and requested permission from the government to establish a national lottery which was organized by Father Bernard. Construction began on September 11, 1853, with Bishop Eugène de Mazenod laying the cornerstone with the deputy mayor of Marseilles in front of a crowd of a few hundred thousand people including fifty bishops and cardinals.

The crypt of the church was completed in 1858 while Eugène was still alive, but he did not live to see the building's completion and dedication in 1864.

Reforms

Despite the objections of his priests, Eugène's plan to require priests to live in community was slowly implemented. He also improved the quality of priests in his diocese by instructing the priests already in his diocese on how to be better pastors and preachers and by giving the responsibility of training new priests for his diocese to the Missionary Oblates of Mary Immaculate.

Unfortunately, following the death of Bishop Eugène de Mazenod, most of the reforms he implemented and the institutions he founded were dismantled during the four-year episcopacy that followed his twenty-four-year episcopacy. After Eugène's death, those who were opposed to his ideas and reforms began to undo what he had done. They even went so far as to remove the oblates from the seminary where they had been training priests for the Diocese of Marseilles. The bishop who replaced Bishop de Mazenod was declared mentally ill after four years in the See of Marseilles and removed from his position. In the wake of this, the priests of Marseilles appointed as vicars of the diocese three men who had held those positions during Bishop de Mazenod's episcopacy. Sadly, by that time, the damage had been done.

The Bishop and the Government

A Thorn

While the people of Marseilles loved their bishop, the same could not be said for the government of France. No matter which political system or regime was in power, they all seemed to clash with Saint Eugène de Mazenod who ferociously fought every move that was made against the Church.

Eugène refused to be bullied by those in power. The government once tried to force the Church to move a cross from the public square of Marseilles into one of the churches. He refused, declaring, "I would rather die than take part in such an apostasy." On another occasion, the government attempted to expel the recently revived Society of Jesus from France. Eugène de Mazenod, who greatly admired the Jesuits because of the influence of Don Bartolo Zinelli, had played a major role in their return to France and did not want to sit idly by as they were forced to leave again, stating, "It is I who brought them here, and it is from me alone they receive their mission and the powers which they exercise the holy ministry. I congratulate myself on having them." His efforts to keep the Jesuits safe were supported by the fishwives who stood guard outside the episcopal residence where some Jesuits were being housed.

Defender and Promoter of Catholic Education

During the lifetime of Saint Eugène de Mazenod, the government frequently infringed upon the rights of the Church to establish schools and other means of educating children in the Catholic Faith. Eugène could not stand to see this occur:

> Others may be able to develop a youth's intelligence with some degree of success, embellish his mind with useful knowledge, polish it, give it a finish, and make it susceptible to all the forms of art; but to seize his heart and cultivate it fruitfully, to root out evil from it and deposit in it the seeds of virtue, to mold his character and temper it with all the virtues that make for a happy and honorable life; no one can accomplish that unless he is inspired with the principles and sentiments of Faith, keeps constantly under the influence of the Church, and fecundates with her teachings the instruction he imparts.

Saint Eugène knew the importance of educating children in the Faith. He had seen what the lack of religious instruction had done in his own life and during the French Revolution and despised the idea of this occurring to a new generation of Catholics. There could be no other option for Eugène, but to defend the Church's right to educate children, and he did so using any means necessary.

Eugène and His Brother Bishops

Eugène's efforts to thwart the government's infringement on Catholicism did not go unnoticed by the other bishops of France. They praised him for his ability to make the Church loved by the people, but his inability to compromise and his fiery personality made them uneasy. Bishop de Mazenod frequently wrote in the press in defense of the Church. His outspokenness often perturbed his brother bishops in France, but he strongly defended the use of the press, writing, "When the arena is the Press, we are in our place in having recourse to the Press...the Press is the greatest means by which we can make our voices heard." Regardless of the reservations they had about his methods, the bishops of France began to respect Eugène de Mazenod and often sought his advice, especially when it came to standing up for the Church. The character Eugène displayed when defending the Church not only impressed his brother bishops, but some more unlikely individuals as well.

Napoleon III

The most unusual individual who came to admire Saint Eugène de Mazenod was Napoleon III. In 1856, the self-proclaimed emperor rewarded Eugène for his character by naming him a Senator. "Lo and behold, I am embarked on a new career, apparently by the will of God; certainly, it is one at which I was not aiming," Eugène wrote of the honor. He took the responsibility seriously, attending the Senate sessions from January until Holy Week and returning for the closing session in June.

The friendship of Saint Eugène and Napoleon III became tested when the latter aligned France against the Papal States. Eugène de Mazenod tried using his power as Senator to force the emperor to honor his agreement with the Pope to be an ally of the Papal States, but was unsuccessful. This controversy between France and Rome prevented Eugène from being elevated to the cardinalate.

While Emperor Napoleon III had no taste for religion, he nevertheless took great pride in seeing members of his own country receive honors within the Church. His admiration and respect for Eugène de Mazenod inspired him to request in 1859 that the bishop of Marseilles be named a cardinal. Pope Pius IX agreed with Napoleon III that the bishop in question ought to become a cardinal, but it sadly did not come to pass. Due to the aforementioned betrayal, the Pope had ceased naming Frenchmen to the cardinalate. This meant Saint Eugène de Mazenod would not become a cardinal as he had been promised. While disappointed, Eugène knew and understood the Holy Father's reasons for not naming him a cardinal. He instead focused, not on rewards and honors on earth, but on the rewards granted by the heavenly Father. "After all, it is all the same whether one is buried in a red cassock or a purple one; the main thing is that the bishop gets to heaven," Eugène stated.

Knowing the Importance of the Affairs of the State

One of the more unusual acts of Bishop Eugène de Mazenod was the dispensation from Mass he gave to the people of Marseilles for Easter Sunday 1848. In that particular year, the Second French Republic had just established itself, and for the first time in France's history, there was universal male suffrage. The bishop of Marseilles allowed his flock to miss Mass that Sunday if it prevented them from voting.

Eugène knew that Catholics have a duty to participate in the governance of their country, and he wished to make that clear to his flock. It may seem strange that he would allow Catholics to miss Easter Mass, but as a former political refugee, Eugène knew what could happen when good people did not help put other virtuous people into political office. He wanted his people to have a say in who was to lead their country.

Gate to the World

The State of the Oblates

While bishop of Marseilles, Eugène de Mazenod remained superior general of the Oblates. Although the administration of both the diocese and the Oblates took a great deal of time, Eugène was able to budget his time wisely. He took over the See of Marseilles twenty-one years after starting the Missionary Oblates, but by that time, its numbers had only grown to forty-two professed religious, despite the fact that over two hundred men had entered the novitiate. Its total number of houses totaled ten, and its founder's ardent desire for foreign missions had not been realized.

Eugène de Mazenod had long desired to see his missionaries spread out all over the world. His attraction to the missionary field dates back to his time in Venice. Shortly after his First Communion, he began to read *Les lettres édifiantes sur les missions de la Chine et du Japon*. The stories of missionaries to Asia inspired in him a desire to convert nonbelievers in foreign lands. When he followed the call to the priesthood, he did not join or form a group of missionaries with a goal of converting souls in foreign lands because he saw the great need for missionaries within his own country.

Yet, the idea of sending his oblates to foreign lands appealed to him. As their superior general, he had attempted to send his oblates to Algeria and to America, but those efforts had failed.

It would not be until he received a visitor from the Western Hemisphere that he would be able to send men overseas.

A Need in Montreal

In 1841, Ignace Bourget, bishop of Montreal, made a journey to Rome. One of the main reasons he traveled to Europe was to find priests from a religious order to serve in his diocese. Along the way, he described the great need his diocese had for priests in the Diocese of Montreal, and one individual to whom he spoke told him to go to the bishop of Marseilles to ask for members of the Missionary Oblates of Mary Immaculate and emphasize that it was for the salvation of souls that the priests were needed. For, if he is told that it is for the salvation of souls, Bishop Bourget was told, he will not be able to refuse.

The suggestion given to Bishop Bourget proved to be sound advice. For, when he explained to Saint Eugène de Mazenod the great need for priests to save souls in Canada, the bishop of Marseilles expressed a keen interest in sending his men to Bourget's diocese. First, though, he needed to consult with his oblates, not wanting to agree to something that drastic without their consent. The oblates enthusiastically agreed, and Eugène chose several of his best men to go to Canada. It saddened him to be separated from them, but Eugène took comfort in knowing that they were doing God's work, that they could be united through the Eucharist, and that this could be the start of something grand for the Missionary Oblates of Mary Immaculate. In one letter to those chosen for the mission, he wrote, "Montreal may be the gate through which our society will go to the whole world."

To All Corners of the World

Bishop de Mazenod's words turned out to be prophetic, for calls for oblates soon began to come from all over the world, including Oregon, Texas, Sri Lanka, South Africa, Ottawa, Buffalo, Pittsburgh, Moose Factory, and many others. However,

Eugène was not interested in going where other religious orders were already operating; he desired to go to the most abandoned places, echoing the sentiment he expressed in his early days of serving the most abandoned in the city of Aix. He and his oblates were now serving the most abandoned throughout the entire world. When Eugène chose missionaries for these endeavors, he always chose, not those whom he could easily do without in France, but the best of his oblates, for he knew the importance of these missions.

Even with all of the work he did in France, Eugène de Mazenod still found time to write to his overseas oblates. The number of letters he wrote to oblates all over the world is staggering. How he found the time to write them so often can only be attributed to the grace of God. Eugène even chided his oblates for not writing him often enough. To one group of oblates, who were in another part of France preparing to go overseas but had not been writing to their superior with agreed-upon frequency, he wrote, "Why haven't you written me, first from Lyons and then from Paris where you have been for several days? That is a bad way to begin your correspondence which we agreed would be very punctual. Father Guibert will reproach you on my behalf. Don't be peeved; you deserve it." This outburst exhibits his parental love for his oblates and his thirst for knowledge of their activities.

In 1857, a priest who had founded the Sisters of the Holy Family of Bordeaux suggested to Bishop de Mazenod that the sisters should be affiliated with the oblates. The superior general accepted, and from thenceforth, whenever the oblates opened up a new field of ministry, the sisters followed behind to complete the work.

A Joyous Father

Saint Eugène de Mazenod watched with great pride as his missionary society, which began in a dilapidated church and convent, grew enormous and spread throughout the world. The

Missionary Oblates of Mary Immaculate had gained prominence, and this resulted in some of his oblates being named to the episcopacy. Eugène took special pleasure in consecrating his spiritual sons.

On Christmas Day 1856, Eugène celebrated Mass with two of the oblates whom he had consecrated as bishops. "It was really a touching sight for Christian hearts to see gathered at the foot of the holy altar, on this beautiful feast, two bishops coming from the ends of the earth to join in public prayer with the pontiff who consecrated them, and offer to God in their person the homage of nations so far apart," he wrote of the occasion.

Son of Mary

Eugène's Mother

During his episcopacy, Bishop Eugène de Mazenod suffered the loss of his mother. In 1851, Marie-Rose passed away at the age of ninety-one. Eugène and his mother may have had a difficult relationship at times, but one thing is clear: Eugène genuinely loved his mother. Marie-Rose, for her part, expressed affection for her son in her letters and took certain actions specifically for his welfare. Trying to arrange a marriage for him was not merely a way to control his life, but a way to ensure his financial security. She was also faithful to attendance of ceremonies at her local parish, her daily recitation of the Little Office of the Virgin Mary, and her devotion to the Immaculate Conception. Her devotion to the Blessed Virgin Mary was one she shared with Eugène who was undoubtedly a son of Mary.

The Influence of Mary on Saint Eugène de Mazenod

During his life and especially during his episcopacy, Saint Eugène de Mazenod did not focus on the written word. "I am not a bishop to write books," he wrote just prior to becoming the bishop of Marseilles. Indeed, the entirety of his priesthood was focused on action and service to the most abandoned. Therefore, it is not by his written words that the influence of the Virgin Mary had on his life can be determined, but rather by how he lived. It is clear by his life that he was greatly influenced by the Blessed Virgin Mary.

Through Mary, Eugène learned obedience. While studying under the tutelage of Don Bartolo Zinelli, Eugène prayed the Little Office of the Blessed Virgin Mary every day. This devotion created an opportunity for reflection on the life of the Blessed Mother. One event of her life that clearly had an influence on his life was her fiat, her yes to the will of God: "Behold, I am the handmaid of the Lord. May it be done to me according to your word."[76] Mary's fiat provided Eugène with a wonderful example of accepting the Lord's will each and every day. "Open to the Spirit, [Mary] consecrated herself totally as lowly handmaid to the person and work of the Savior," he wrote. "She received Christ in order to share Him with all the world whose hope He is. In her, we recognize the model of the Church's faith and our own." In Eugène's mind, Mary exemplified obedience to the Lord's will.

Moreover, Eugène instructed his oblates to bring Mary with them into the missionary field. "Bear in mind that to propagate devotion to [Mary] everywhere is a special duty of our vocation," he wrote. The oblates entered the missionary field using Mary to draw others to Christ. "In the joys and sorrows of our missionary life, we feel close to her who is the Mother of Mercy," Eugène said. "Wherever our ministry takes us, we will strive to instill genuine devotion to the Immaculate Virgin who prefigured God's final victory over evil." To Eugène, missionary work without the assistance of the Mother of God was unthinkable.

Eugène also knew the importance of spreading the devotion to Mary in France. In his pastoral letters on the Virgin Mary, it is clear he viewed honoring her as a necessary part of the Christian life:

> Next to that which directly concerns God, nothing is more precious for truly enlightened piety than that which concerns the honor of the Blessed Virgin Mary. Here we

---

[76] Luke 1:38.

encounter all that exists in a son towards his mother. And what a Mother! To us she gave her Son, the world's life and salvation; she engendered all of us spiritually at the foot of the Cross through the pangs of the passion and death of the God-Man, the blessed fruit of her womb. She is rightly called the new Eve and the co-redemptrix of the human race.

At times, his writing might seem like he viewed her as a goddess or a fourth member of the Trinity. Statements like "[Mary] is the dawn of our Redemption, the ineffable moment when the promises began to be fulfilled" make it seem she is the Savior, not Jesus, but Eugène knew who she was and that there were limits to the honor due to Mary. He wrote, "We never give too much honor to the Blessed Virgin provided devotion to her is understood and practiced in the limited sense of what is due to a creature, however great and sublime she may be." He knew she should be honored, not worshipped. Christians should not worship her, but they should honor her and seek her intercession.

Eugène knew and stressed that Mary's glory is actually the glory of God shining through her, stating, "God's own glory is enhanced in Mary." To honor Mary, in Saint Eugène's mind, is to honor Jesus. "It is the Son whom we honor in the person of the Mother and that is why, in our homage to Mary, it is impossible to overstep the limit, provided we consider her a creature, because God then always remains the supreme end of all that homage," he wrote.

It was that attitude of desiring her intercession that Eugène carried with him in his service to the most abandoned. It is clear his Marian spirituality played a major role in her service to others. When a hospital was named for Mary, he was overjoyed, stating, "The patroness of this asylum of suffering is the one who is called Mother of Sorrow, the Solace of the Afflicted, and the Health of the Sick. Short of Jesus on the Cross, no more consoling vision could be presented to the patients."

The Blessed Virgin's Special Grace

On the Feast of the Assumption in 1822, Eugène de Mazenod was praying before a statue of the Blessed Virgin, when something unusual occurred. No one is entirely sure what happened, and Eugène himself did not go into great detail when he described the incident in a letter to Father Henri Tempier. There is a tradition that claims the statue moved, and the head of Mary inclined towards him. However, neither Eugène de Mazenod nor any primary documents make that claim. What Eugène told Father Henri Tempier is the following:

> Would that I could share with you all that I experienced in the way of consolation on this beautiful day devoted to Mary our Queen! I had not felt for a long time as much joy in speaking of her grandeur and in encouraging our Christians to put all their confidence in her, as during my instruction to the Sodality this morning. I can safely hope I was understood and I can well believe that all the faithful who came to our church this evening shared the fervor with which I was inspired at the sight of the statue of the Holy Virgin and greater still by the graces which she obtained from her divine Son, I dare say, while we were invoking her with so much affection, because she is our Mother. I believe I owe to her also a special experience that I felt today, I will not go so far as to say more than ever, but certainly more than usual. I cannot describe it too well because it comprised several things but all related, however, to a single object, our dear Society. It seemed to me that what I saw, what I could put my finger on, was that within her lies hidden the germ of very great virtues, and that she can achieve infinite good; I found her worthy, everything pleased me about her, I cherished her rules, her statutes; her

ministry seemed sublime to me, as it is indeed. I found in her bosom sure means of salvation, even infallible, such is how they looked to me.

We will never know the full extent of what occurred in the soul of Saint Eugène de Mazenod on August 15, 1822, but what is clear is that he felt something incredible. The source of the grace was the intercession of the Blessed Virgin Mary. Despite not bearing her name yet, the religious order founded by Eugène de Mazenod was under her guidance and protection. When one considers this event, it is clear that the life of Saint Eugène and that of his Congregation was heavily influenced by the Mother of God.

There is evidence to suggest that Eugène de Mazenod consciously knew of the Blessed Virgin's special relationship with his missionary society prior to being given the name Missionary Oblates of Mary Immaculate. During his audience with Pope Leo XII to ask for papal approbation of his Congregation, he asked whether or not they should change their name a second time. The name he suggested instead of Oblates of Saint Charles was "Oblates of the Most Holy and Immaculate Virgin Mary." Saint Charles had been his patron saint since birth, but the name did not seem right. Perhaps, the events of August 15, 1822, gave him some sense that the Blessed Virgin Mary was instrumental to the success of his society's endeavors. When he learned that the Pope had given them the name "The Missionary Oblates of Mary Immaculate, conceived without sin," Eugène called the name "a passport to Heaven."

The Immaculate Conception

The French had long been firm believers in the Immaculate Conception of Mary, the Mother of God. When Pius IX began considering proclaiming the Immaculate Conception as infallible dogma, Bishop Eugène de Mazenod became one of the most vocal supporters of the proclamation. He wrote to the

Holy Father in 1849, five years before the dogma was defined, imploring him to proclaim Mary's Immaculate Conception as infallibly true:

> [It is the] ardor of everyone's desire at last to see a definitive and solemn decree from the Apostolic See stating that the Most Holy Mother of God, the loving Mother of us all, the Immaculate Virgin Mary, was conceived without original sin. The members of the Congregation of the Oblates of the Most Holy and Immaculate Virgin Mary felt an immense joy impossible to describe.
>
> ... For many centuries, Most Holy Father, the Church of Marseilles, the oldest in all of Gaul, has taken pride in professing the pious belief in the Immaculate Conception of the Blessed Virgin...
>
> The clergy of my diocese was always faithfully attached to the doctrine of the Immaculate Conception of Mary.... As for my personal opinion as a bishop of the Church of God, happily called to speak on the question at hand, with the help of the Holy Spirit and the protection of the Mother of the Eternal Light, I say without a doubt that: deeply rooted in the tradition of the Church entrusted to me, in the opinion of the most authoritative theologians and of the most virtuous and the holiest persons of our times and given the theological reasons that—for the honor of the Mother of God and her divine Son—call for the total absence of sin in this most excellent and beloved Mother of God, I say that it is to be held and defined as a dogma of the Catholic faith that the Blessed Virgin Mary was conceived without sin. I express this feeling with a burning desire to see it finally adopted by Your Holiness and taught infallibly to the whole Church of God with the supreme authority granted on the earth by Christ to Peter.

In 1854, Bishop de Mazenod was present for the official proclamation of the dogma. He described the occasion, saying "every eye was filled with tears and all hearts were on fire like those of the disciples at Emmaus on hearing the words of the Divine Master. At that moment, one had the feeling the heavens were opening, and that by fulfilling His infallible promises, Jesus Christ was sending to His Church the Paraclete who was coming, who was there, and who was speaking through the mouth of him whose 'faith must never fail.'" While in Rome for this momentous occasion, he declared, "My heart overflowed with Catholicism." This occasion brought him so much joy that he requested to be buried in the miter he wore that day.

Son of Mary to the End

In his spiritual will and testament, Eugène wrote:

> I invoke the intercession of the Most Holy and Immaculate Virgin Mary, Mother of God, daring to remind her in all humility, but with consolation, of the filial devotedness of my whole life and the desire I have always had of making her known and loved, and of spreading her worship in every land through the ministry of those whom the Church has given me as my children.

The above writing testifies to Eugène's lifelong devotion to Mary. He calls this a filial devotion, that of a son to a mother. Eugène even chided himself for not calling upon her more often. This sentiment is expressed in a prayer he wrote to Mary:

> Virgin Mary, my good Mother, if I called upon you more often I would have less cause to groan inwardly. Help me, O my Mother, by your powerful intercession to carry out better than I have until now, all the obligations your dear Son imposed upon me so that, with your help, my reward is to conscientiously carry them out. And as I grow less

unworthy, I promise to strive toward and to enter into the still greater reward that awaits me in Heaven.

Some historians and scholars downplay Eugène's devotion to the Mother of God, but this is an error. There is no denying there are few overt references to the influence of Mary in the writings of Eugène de Mazenod. However, it is clear, if a careful examination of his life is made, that Saint Eugène de Mazenod loved and strove to imitate the Blessed Virgin, especially in her acceptance of the Lord's will. His retreat notes mention maintaining daily devotions to Mary, and the Blessed Virgin was the patroness of his youth group in Aix[77] and his religious order. Throughout Eugène's life, Mary can be found covertly guiding him towards her Son.

---

[77] "From the moment they entered the Congregation, they took this holy Mother of God as their advocate and patron; the devotion they will have for her will be their safeguard," Eugène wrote, describing Mary's role in the youth association. Furthermore, he instructed the boys to pray the Little Office of the Blessed Virgin Mary every day.

Death

On the evening of Pentecost Sunday 1861, the old bishop laid on his bed. A crowd of individuals whom he deeply loved were gathered around him. They knew there was not much time left. Over the past few months, a wound on his side had been slowly sucking his life away. The wound had mystified the doctors who examined him. One doctor, not knowing what else to do, stuck his finger in the wound to see if he could feel anything that would give an indication of the ailment. Instead of wincing at the pain, the bishop jokingly compared the doctor to the Apostle Thomas probing the wounds of the Risen Christ.

The previous night, May 20, Father Henri Tempier, his best friend and right-hand man for the previous forty-seven years, had informed him that the doctors had failed to find an explanation for his ailment and that the mysterious wound would soon finish tormenting him. It was time to prepare for the end. The ailing bishop requested his cross and his Rosary. "These are my weapons," he declared and did not let them go until he let go of his spirit. He also made the unusual request of being awake for his death. "If I should doze off and you see that things are getting worse, please wake me up," he said. "I want to die knowing that I am dying."

Some priests of his diocese and some members of the religious order he founded began visiting him, to say farewell and to soak up any last bits of wisdom the bishop might share with them. Upon hearing their request for one last message from their spiritual father, he said, "I die happy because God deigned to choose me to found in the Church the Congregation of the Oblates. Among yourselves practice charity, charity, charity; and outside, zeal for the salvation of souls." A telegram had been sent to the Pope asking for a blessing from Rome. Hours later, a response arrived stating the request had been granted. There was nothing left to do, but pray.

Prayers were said throughout the night and the next day. As it was Pentecost Sunday, the bishop requested one of his younger priests to recite the Sequence of the Mass of the Holy Spirit. The young man obeyed his superior and began the recitation. Due to this priest's lack of experience and the seriousness of the situation, the young priest occasionally forgot some of the words. When he did so, the dying bishop was quick to come to his aid and provide the forgotten word or phrase.

In the final moments of his life, the bishop was surrounded by his spiritual children praying the Salve Regina. As the prayer concluded, "O clement! O loving! O sweet Virgin Mary!" he gestured towards Heaven with each invocation. Then, he gave his spirit to the Lord.

His friends and coworkers in the vineyard of the Lord sprinkled holy water on his body and stayed for a long time, praying and crying. Yet, they were happy because God had allowed them the grace of witnessing the peaceful death of a holy man, one who overcame his own shortcomings, political exile, a broken family, and uncertainty with respect to his place in the world to found a religious order, serve as bishop of Marseilles, and share in the Beatific Vision, Saint Eugène de Mazenod.

Canonization

Eugène de Mazenod had a passionate love of Jesus Christ, and was devoted without reservation to the Church!...This Pastor and Founder, an authentic witness of the Holy Spirit, launches a fundamental call to all the baptized and to all of today's apostles: let yourselves be filled by the fire of Pentecost and you will have missionary enthusiasm.

Pope Paul VI, spoke the words above on October 19, 1975, the day he beatified Eugène de Mazenod, almost five years after he had declared him venerable. This beatification meant that the heroic virtue of Eugène's life had been accepted and now only a miracle was needed for his canonization to go forward. This miracle would occur twelve years later in Mexico.

Jesús Hernández Serrano, a fifty-five-year-old truck driver living in the Ampliación Providencia district of Mexico City, grew ill in March of 1987. His symptoms included stomach aches, bloating, loss of appetite, and fevers. He thought it was something he ate at a party or something that would go away if he quit drinking. After six weeks and losing fifty pounds, he checked into a hospital. Tests for Hepatitis B and salmonella infections turned up negative, and a liver biopsy was performed. The results were not good. Jesús was diagnosed with a rare and aggressive form of liver cancer. Doctors estimated he would die within months. The Serranos did not have enough money to pay for an elongated hospital stay, and the decision was made to let him live out his finals months peacefully at home.

Jesús was Catholic, but did not take his faith seriously. The parish his family attended was served by the Missionary Oblates of Mary Immaculate. Two oblate priests came to his home to give him the Anointing of the Sick and suggested a novena to Blessed Eugène de Mazenod. From June 7 until the night of June 16, the Serranos' fellow parishioners joined them in praying for healing. The morning after the ninth day, Jesús woke up and felt no pain, despite having been in excruciating pain for the nine days of the novena. A nurse that had been to see him the final night of the novena thought for certain he would not make it through the night, but she was shocked the next day to see him out of bed and walking around.

Over the next few days, his appetite returned, he regained his weight, and he returned to work. Jesús thought perhaps the illness would come back, so when his daughter gave him her bonus check as a Christmas gift, he used the money for medical tests. The results showed no sign of cancer.

The oblates reported the event to their superiors. The report led to an official examination from the Vatican. After years of investigation and medical tests, five medical experts concluded on March 24, 1994, that the healing could not be explained by medicine or any other scientific explanation. Blessed Eugène de Mazenod's intercession had worked a miracle.

Pope John Paul II canonized Eugène de Mazenod on December 3, 1995. The Pope who is now a saint himself declared on that day:

> Eugène de Mazenod was one of those apostles who prepared the modern times, our times. Proclaiming Christ for him meant becoming the fully apostolic man which every age needs, filled with that fervor and missionary zeal that gradually configured him to the risen Christ. He led the faithful to accept Christ with an ever more generous faith,

so that they could live fully their vocation as children of God. His influence is not limited to the times in which he lived, but continues even in our time. For the good accomplished by virtue of the Holy Spirit does not perish, but endures in every "now" of history. Thanks be to God!

Epilogue: A Saint for Today

Saint Thérèse of Lisieux said, "I will spend my heaven doing good on earth. I will let fall a shower of roses." In a similar proclamation, Saint Teresa of Calcutta wrote, "If I ever become a saint—I will surely be one of 'darkness.' I will continually be absent from heaven—to light the light of those in darkness on earth." Both statements indicate how these two saints intended to intercede from Heaven. Saint Eugène de Mazenod did not leave a declaration as these two did. Yet, if the lives of both Saint Thérèse of Lisieux and Saint Teresa of Calcutta are examined, it should come as no surprise that these two saints would choose to intercede from Heaven in this manner, for this is how they interceded for others during their lives. Therefore, if we want to know how Saint Eugène de Mazenod wishes to intercede from Heaven, an examination of his life will yield an answer.

The goal of Saint Eugène's life on earth was and is now in Heaven to serve the most abandoned in the world and to save souls. The strategy Eugène employed in reaching out to the abandoned was to recognize their humanity, first and foremost. Then, he would go about converting them. "We must lead men to act like human beings, first of all, and then like Christians, and, finally, we must help them to become saints," he taught his oblates. Thus, in examining the life of Saint Eugène de Mazenod and seeking his intercession, a person will relate to the struggles of his life and see that this saint is a human being, too. As Pope Paul VI said, "We want to discover in saints whatever brings them closer to us, rather than what sets them apart. We want to put them at our level as human beings…That way, we stand the chance of having confidence in them—we can share with them the common and burdensome state of our earthly experience." Saint Eugène wants to empathize with our burdens, for he, too, experienced burdens.

In the life of Saint Eugène, a multitude of persons can find something to which they can relate. The problems plaguing the world today are the same problems with which Eugène dealt in his day. People still struggle with anger, causing divisions and hurt feelings. Families still find themselves becoming refugees, placing many in foreign lands without their consent. The divorce rate remains high, causing grief for children who have done no wrong and inspiring animosity between spouses. Governments continue to threaten the open practice of religion, forcing many to fear that their way of life might soon be jeopardized. Prisoners are still shunned, denying the opportunity for forgiveness. Religious education continues to be inadequate, perpetuating ignorance of the true teachings of the Church. The poor remain, plagued by starvation and other anxieties. Some priests still fail to develop proper preaching skills, leaving many of the faithful without spiritual guidance. Faith continues to be forced out of the public square, further secularizing the culture.

Yet, no person who suffers from any of the issues mentioned above need be defined by their struggles. Saint Eugène refused to let the pains of his youth stop him from realizing the Lord's plan for him, and the problems he faced as an adult could not stop him from carrying out his ministry. All who feel abandoned can look to Saint Eugène and his example of not being defined by the struggles he endured. Eugène knew who he was in the eyes of the Lord, and he desires to help everyone make the same discovery today:

Come, then, and learn what you are in the eyes of God... [A]ll you who are burdened with misery...listen to me! You are the children of God, the brothers of Jesus Christ, co-heirs of His eternal kingdom, the cherished portion of His inheritance...There is an immortal soul within you, made to the image of God Whom it is destined to possess one day; a soul redeemed at the price of the Blood of Jesus Christ, more precious in the eyes of God than all the riches of the earth, than all the kingdoms of the world; a soul He considers more desirable than the government of the entire universe.

Through relating to Saint Eugène, we encounter virtue and love. We see our inherent dignity, and we can then draw close to the Lord. From Heaven, Eugène burns with zeal for the salvation of our souls. His intercession can help us act like humans, then Christians, and finally become saints.

Appendix: Prayers

Miscellaneous Prayers
Composed by Saint Eugène de Mazenod between 1806–1808?

A.) On rising in the morning.
Nox praecessit, dies appropinquavit, abjiciamus opera tenebrarum. Rom. 13 [:12] [The night is almost over, it will be daylight soon—let us give up all the things we prefer to do under cover of the dark.] Open, my God, my heart to your love as my eyes open to the daylight; it is by your grace that I begin this day, do not let me to spend it in empty amusements. Alas! the time you give me cost the blood of your son, would I be so wretched as not to consecrate it entirely to your service? *Mane astabo tibi, mane exaudies vocem meam.* Psalm 5 [:3] [At daybreak you listen for my voice; and at dawn I hold myself in readiness for you.]

B.) While dressing.
Induimini Dominum nostrum Jesum Christum. Romans 13 [:14] [Let your armour be the Lord Jesus Christ.] May these clothes truly serve to keep me mindful, my God, of my lost innocence.... Will what should be source of shame for me be one of pride and vanity?

C.) For a perfect conversion.

How still imperfect, my God, is my conversion; the root of sin lives on in me; the thoughts and memory of the world are still powerfully at work; the things I have renounced retain their hold on my imagination, and reawaken baleful images. My heart, still weak, is quite disturbed by it, and in the midst of this disturbance it feels all its passions coming back to life; it takes but little for it to be ensnared. Is this what it is to be perfectly God's? My inconstancy in the little good I do, my God, is no less humiliating to me; full of good desires, I am often satisfied with their formulation, almost all my zeal is used up in the making of plans; I fluctuate between yielding to grace and to my own desires, while time flows by, I journey swiftly towards eternity, and I am always the same. Shall I all my life be the plaything of the enemy of my salvation? Make firm, my God, my inconstancy, wholly change my heart; inspire within me, for my salvation, the same zeal I showed for my damnation. *Sicut exhibuistis membra vestra servire iniquitati, ita nunc exhibete servire justitiae.* Romans 6 [:19] [As once you put your bodies at the service of vice and immorality, so now you must put them at the service of righteousness....]

D.) Against relapsing into sin.

Have I come back to you, my God, only to burden myself with the greater crime of falling back into sin? In all conscience, is my ingratitude to match the greatness of your love? Am I to meet all your bounty with but a new tissue of sins? My God, shorten the course of my life, rather than permit the demon to reenter my heart. Can I hide from how awful such a state would be, my God, after what you have yourself made known to us in the Gospel? A sinner who is still unconverted is in the power of but a single demon, but a sinner who relapses lets a legion of impure spirits into his soul...Even so on the pretext of a necessary break, I yield too much to my senses, pleasure and dissipation; I allow myself to be led too much by my vivacity;

I do not take adequate precautions against my concupiscence, the impressions of the world, the devil's wiles, I do not watch enough over myself, over the danger to which I am exposed. A perilous state for salvation. Open my eyes to the danger, my God; reawaken my zeal, strengthen my faith: terrified by the danger to which I am exposed, sustained by the power of your grace, I will bemoan my condition; I will pray with more ardour; I will redouble my vigilance so as to work efficaciously for my salvation. *Spiritu meo in praecordiis meis de mane vigilabo ad te.* Isaiah 26 [:9] [At night my soul longs for you and my spirit in me seeks for you.]

Marian Prayer
Composed by Saint Eugène de Mazenod on October 30, 1818.

Virgin Mary, my good Mother, if I called upon you more often I would have less cause to groan inwardly. Help me, O my Mother, by your powerful intercession to carry out better than I have until now, all the obligations your dear Son imposed upon me so that, with your help, my reward is to conscientiously carry them out. And as I grow less unworthy, I promise to strive toward and to enter into the still greater reward that awaits me in Heaven.

Prayer to Jesus to Grow in Love
*Composed by Saint Eugène de Mazenod in 1811
just prior to his ordination.*

O Jesus, look with compassion
Upon your poor servant.
It seems to me that I do love You,
But I am afraid of deceiving myself.

I feel that, were you to question me
As you once requested the Prince of the Apostles…
I would answer, "Yes, Lord, I love You,"
But You would not have to ask me three times
To make me uneasy about the love I pledged to You.
I repeat, I am afraid of deceiving myself.

I do indeed believe that I love You,
But You, the uncreated Light,
You penetrate the hidden recesses of my heart,
You can read all its secrets;
You sound the depths of every human heart,
And perhaps You see that I do not really love You.

O, my Savior, my Father, my Love,
Make me love You
I do not ask for any other thing—
Because to love You is everything.

Grant that I may love You.

A Prayer to One's Guardian Angel
Written by Saint Eugène de Mazenod as a suggestion for his sister, Ninette, when she found herself in moments of temptation.

My good angel, my body may be here, but my heart is with God. You who are constantly at the foot of God's throne, offer Him my intentions, tell Him that I love Him above all things. Amen.

Litany to Saint Eugène de Mazenod, Intercessor for Families in Need
Taken from eugenedemazenod.net

Response to each invocation: St. Eugène de Mazenod, lead us to Jesus through the trials of life.

1.) You who were rich and content at birth but afflicted by poverty and suffering very early in life. **R/**

2.) You were in exile for the safety of life in face of the terrors of the French Revolution. **R/**

3.) You lost everything in exile but were miraculously sustained by God's providence. **R/**

4.) You were deprived of education in exile but God sent you Fr. Bartolo Zinelli in Venice to guide your path. **R/**

5.) When your parents were separated, you lost the warmth and love of your mother at a tender age but you were blessed with the loving presence of our heavenly Mother. **R/**

6.) Having failed in all your attempts to reconcile your parents, you experienced utter helplessness. **R/**

7.) You were lonely and had no hope of a bright future in the prime of your youth and thus, you experienced the depression of the idle youth. **R/**

8.) When you returned to your motherland at the age of twenty you were showered with all the pleasures of worldly life and you were quick to discern their vanity. **R/**

9.) You encountered the crucified Christ on a Good Friday and were awakened to the immeasurable love of the Savior. **R/**

10.) At the foot of the Cross, on that Good Friday, you realized God's wonderful plan for you. **R/**

11.) You gave yourself to the service of the Church and dedicated your priestly life to serve the young and the most abandoned. **R/**

12.) In your passionate love for the poor you founded the Congregation of the Missionary Oblates of Mary Immaculate. **R/**

13.) With your generous heart embracing the whole world, you sent your missionaries to the ends of the world. **R/**

14.) Called to serve as the Bishop of Marseilles, you touched the hearts of God's people. **R/**

15.) You instructed the members of your Congregation before your death to show each other charity and to work with zeal for the salvation of people. **R/**

16.) You were proclaimed a saint of the Church for the welfare of those in difficulties. **R/**

17.) You mediate before our heavenly Father on behalf of the families that undergo trials and difficulties and you are quick to come to their aid. **R/**

Let us pray:
Almighty and loving God, you led St. Eugène de Mazenod through the sufferings and challenges of a dysfunctional family to a life of holiness. Through his constant intercession bless the children and the youth of broken families. Strengthen the

spouses to strive for unity. Grant them the gifts of understanding, patience, love and courage to overcome the problems of life. We ask this through Jesus Christ our Savior and Lord. **Amen.**

Litany to Saint Eugène de Mazenod for Those in Need
Taken from eugenedemazenod.net

Response to each invocation: St. Eugène, guide us to the Savior in our time of need.

1.) Born into a rich upper-class family, you experienced what it meant to lose everything, your comfort, social position, and friends. Yet you experienced that God our Savior did not abandon you. **R/**

2.) At the age of 7 you experienced revolution, persecution and fear and what it meant to have to run away to save your life. The Savior was with you, and you were protected. **R/**

3.) In exile you experienced living away from your country, culture, language and environment. The Savior helped you to adapt, learn and grow from every event. **R/**

4.) In Venice you did not have the possibility to go to school. The Savior sent you a wonderful personal teacher in Father Bartolo Zinelli who cared for you and gave you the human and religious foundations you needed. **R/**

5.) As a teenager you suffered the break-up of your family and lived without your mother and sister for many years. The Savior comforted you by giving you the understanding of the motherhood of Mary. **R/**

6.) As an adolescent and young man you longed to reconcile your parents, but suffered from the pain of the irreparable separation of your parents and your wish for them never being realized. **R/**

7.) In Naples you experienced the joyless existence of poverty, boredom and lack of hope for the future. The Savior formed you through this so that you could feel with others who suffered in the same situation. **R/**

8.) In Sicily you lived the life of a nobleman again, and pampered yourself, even in making up a noble title and calling yourself "Count de Mazenod." Yet the Savior sent you a guide in the Duchess of Cannizzaro who taught you to become aware of the needs of the poor. **R/**

9.) Returning to France at the age of 20, you gave yourself to a life of frivolity and pleasure. But the Savior led you to understand how empty this was. **R/**

10.) One Good Friday, standing at the foot of the Cross, you experienced the unconditional love of the Savior for you and your life was transformed for ever by His love. **R/**

11.) On that Good Friday, standing at the foot of the Cross, the Savior led you to understand that despite all your sins and guilt, you had been liberated and forgiven and healed. **R/**

12.) On that Good Friday, standing at the foot of the Cross, you were led to understand your vocation to give yourself to the service of your Savior through the gift of your whole life as a priest. **R/**

13.) In a country which had been ravaged by the Revolution, and which had forgotten about God, you were helped by the

Savior to understand that your vocation was to live only for God and to bring others to God's love. **R/**

14.) After your ordination you returned to Aix en Provence and became aware of the cry of the poor. The Savior responded to their suffering through your preaching and service to the poorest classes, to the youth and prisoners. **R/**

15.) Your ministry to the abandoned and dying Austrian prisoners of war led you to the point of death through typhus. Through the fervent and constant prayers of the youth you ministered to, the Savior healed you. **R/**

16.) Impelled by your passionate love for the Savior you invited others to join you in your ministry of preaching to the most abandoned. The Savior used you to bring to birth the Missionary Oblates of Mary Immaculate. **R/**

17.) In order to be "all for God," the Savior invited you and your companions to bind yourselves to Him through religious life, living the vows in apostolic community. **R/**

18.) When you mourned the death of your young Oblate companions, the Savior showed you that they were part of the Oblate community in heaven, and that through their prayers they were fully involved in your mission preaching. **R/**

19.) When the small group of Oblates was endangered by forces threatening to destroy it, you turned in prayer to Mary Immaculate, and in front of her statue you received the assurance that you were doing the will of the Savior. **R/**

20.) At a time when the Church was not recognizing any new religious congregations, the Pope recognized the work of the Savior in what you and the young Oblates were doing, and officially approved the Oblate Congregation. **R/**

21.) Fully committed to the welfare of the Church, you sacrificed yourself and your personal wishes to serve wherever the Savior was calling you. You accepted to be Vicar General of Marseilles and then Bishop so as to better serve the most abandoned. **R/**

22.) The anti-religious activities of the French government caused them to attack you and inflict much suffering on you. You never wavered in the cause of justice and were strengthened in your defense of the Church by the constant grace of the Savior. **R/**

23.) As Bishop of Marseilles you dedicated all your energies to being a loving father to your flock, with a special insistence on mirroring the Savior's love for the poor and most abandoned. **R/**

24.) During the various deadly cholera epidemics you risked your life to minister to the sick and dying, being prepared to die as a martyr of love in imitation of the Savior. **R/**

25.) You experienced the intimate love and closeness of the Savior's presence in the Word of God, you nourished yourself on it each day and led others to the same source of nourishment. **R/**

26.) You experienced the intimate love and closeness of the Savior's presence in the Eucharist, and taught and encouraged all those you ministered to, to have a strong Eucharistic devotion. **R/**

27.) When you became aware of the cry of the poor in distant countries because they did not know the Savior, you sent your Oblate sons to bring them the good news of the Savior's unconditional love for them. **R/**

28.) Your last testament to your Oblate sons was what the Savior had taught you throughout your life: "charity, charity, charity among yourselves, and outside, zeal for the salvation of souls." **R/**

29.) You always made Mary Immaculate known and loved as a mother who leads those in need to the Savior. The Savior crowned your life by calling you to Himself during the praying of the Salve Regina. **R/**

30.) In your canonization the Church recognized your sanctity and proclaimed you to be a model for others to follow in their search for Christ the Savior. As a saint you are a powerful intercessor for all in our poverty and abandonment. R/

31.) Today you continue to be present through the ministry of your Oblate missionaries and their associates throughout the world. Make them fearless and generous in their ministry to all who search for the meaning in their lives that only the Savior can bring. **R/**

32.) Let us pause in silence to think of our own personal intentions and requests… **R/**

Let us pray:
Loving Savior, we thank you for the life and intercession of Saint Eugene de Mazenod. Accompanied by his prayers we bring to you all our personal intentions and those of our loved ones, especially the sick and suffering. We ask also that you will inspire many generous persons to follow Saint Eugene's missionary example by dedicating their lives to being the Savior's co-operators like you were. We ask all this with loving confidence. **Amen.**

Bibliography

Aubin, Hervé. *The Founder of the Oblates: Saint Eugène de Mazenod*. Battleford, Saskatchewan: Marian, 1997. Print.

De Mazenod, Eugène. *My Name Is Eugène de Mazenod*. Translated by Francis D. Flanagan. Edited by Herménégilde Charbonneau. Boston: Missionary Oblates of Mary Immaculate, Eastern Province of United States, 1976. Print.

Eugene de Mazenod speaks to us.
http://www.eugenedemazenod.net.

Fillassier, Jean Jacques. *Eraste, ou l'Ami de la jeunesse.*

Hubenig, Alfred, and René Motte. *Living in the Spirit's Fire: Saint Eugene de Mazenod, Founder of the Missionary Oblates of Mary Immaculate*. Toronto, Ontario: Novalis, 1995. Print.

King, Arthur. *"...One Good Friday...": 1807*. Grand Rapids, MI: Oblates of Mary Immaculate, 1996. Print.

Lawrence, Claude V. J. *Every Inch an Apostle: Twelve Portrayals of the Servant of God Eugene de Mazenod, Bishop and Founder O.M.I.* Ottawa: Etudes Oblates with the Collaboration of the C.W.M. (Ceylon), 1947. Print.

Lebrun, François, ed. *Histoire des catholiques en France: Du XVe siecle a nos jours* (history of Catholics in France from the 15th century to our day).

Leflon, Jean. *Eugene de Mazenod Bishop of Marseilles: Founder of the Oblates of Mary Immaculate 1782-1861* (Vol. 1 of 4: *The Steps of a Vocation 1782-1814*). Translated by Francis D. Flanagan. New York: Fordham UP, 1961. Print.

Oblate Communications. http://omiworld.org.

Pielorz, J. *The Spiritual Life of Bishop de Mazenod (1782-1812): A Critical Study*. Diss. Association of Oblate Studies and Research, Rome, 1998.

Roche, Aimé. Eugène de Mazenod: Illustrated Biography. Translated by D. Long. Lyon: Editions Du Chalet, 1961. Print.

About the Author

Alex R. Hey has been featured on TheBatmanUniverse.net, Catholic365.com, EpicPew.com, and in *The Eagle Democrat* (Warren, Arkansas) and *The Argus Leader* (Sioux Falls, South Dakota). His debut collection of poetry, *Poems I Found in My Prayer Journals*, can be found on Amazon.com.

Originally from Maple Grove, Minnesota, Mr. Hey has lived in Sioux Falls, South Dakota, since 1995. His interests include writing, following hockey and Minnesota sports teams, Batman, detective stories, community theater, and improv.

Find him online at alexrhey.com.

About Leonine Publishers

Leonine Publishers LLC makes fine Catholic literature available to Catholics throughout the English-speaking world. Leonine Publishers offers an innovative "hybrid" approach to book publication that helps authors as well as readers. Please visit our web site at www.leoninepublishers.com to learn more about us. Browse our online bookstore to find more solid Catholic titles to uplift, challenge, and inspire.

Our patron and namesake is Pope Leo XIII, a prudent, yet uncompromising pope during the stormy years at the close of the 19th century. Please join us as we ask his intercession for our family of readers and authors.

Do you have a book inside you? Visit our web site today. Leonine Publishers accepts manuscripts from Catholic authors like you. If your book is selected for publication, you will have an active part in the production process. This book is an example of our growing selection of literature for the busy Catholic reader of the 21st century.

www.leoninepublishers.com

www.ingramcontent.com/pod-product-compliance
Lightning Source LLC
Chambersburg PA
CBHW070447050426
42451CB00015B/3372